THE CHANGING FACE OF LONDON
HISTORIC BUILDINGS AND THE CROSSRAIL ROUTE

Richard Brown, Julian Munby, Andy Shelley and Kirsty Smith

with contributions by Anne Dodd and Ian Scott

Graphics by Magdalena Wachnik

Maps by Gary Jones

Published by Oxford Archaeology, Janus House, Oxford

Copyright © Crossrail Ltd 2016

A CIP catalogue record for this book is available from the British Library

Crossrail Archaeology Publication series designed and series-edited by Jay Carver,
Marit Leenstra and Andrew Briffett

Production and design by Oxford Archaeology Graphics Office

Editing by Anne Dodd and Andy Shelley

Copy editing by Ian Scott

Front cover: the geometric staircase at 11-12 Blomfield Street

Typeset by Production Line, Oxford

Printed in the United Kingdom by Henry Ling Limited,
at the Dorset Press, Dorchester, DT1 1HD
an ISO 14001 certified printer

MIX
Paper from
responsible sources
FSC™ C013985

CONTRIBUTORS

Principal authors   **Richard Brown, Julian Munby,**
                                                Andy Shelley and Kirsty Smith

Graphics   Magdalena Wachnik
Maps and Geographic Information Systems   Gary Jones
Project manager (OA)   Richard Brown
Project manager (Ramboll)   Andy Shelley
Post–excavation manager   Anne Dodd

CONTENTS

List of figures vi

Acknowledgements xii

Foreword xiv

1   Introduction 1

      Notes 3

2   Domestic London 5

      London's changing demography 5

      The Georgian housing boom 6

      Victorian London 8

      Crossrail in Soho 9

          No. 94 Dean St

          No. 93 Dean Street

          No. 9 Diadem Court

          No. 5a Great Chapel Street

      Notes 21

3   Commercial London 23

      Introduction 23

      Crossrail and commercial London 26

      Oxford Street and Soho 27

          No. 95 Dean Street and its occupants

          No. 93 Dean Street

          No. 9 Great Chapel Street/No. 4 Fareham Street

      Light industries 33

          Oxford Street and Charing Cross Road

      Notes 38

4   Industrial London 41

      Introduction 41

Electricity 42
    Crossrail and White Hart Depot electricity generating station

Food Production 46
    Smithfield Market
    Crossrail and Smithfield
    Nos 20–23 Long Lane and No.2 Lindsey Street
    No. 3 Lindsey Street
    Nos 8–9 Hayne Street
    Armour and Co
    54–64 Charterhouse Street (Smithfield House)

East End London industries 56
    Artesian well, Anchor Brewery, Mile End Road

Beyond the River Lea 58
    East London Soap Works

Notes 64

5   The rise of the purpose-built office 67

The origins of the office. 68

Crossrail and the office building 69
    Nos 11–12 Blomfield Street
    Nos 9–15 Oxford Street
    No. 2 Fisher Street, Camden
    No. 65 Davies Street
    The modern office block

The layout and organisation of the office and the introduction
of new technology 78

Notes 80

6   London at leisure 81

The public house. 81
    The Bath House
    The Excelsior
    The Barge (formerly The Freemasons Tavern)

The cinema 89
    Astoria Cinema

Notes 91

7 Crossrail's legacy: enhancing and creating places 93

Taking a different approach. 93

The measure of time 95

Gazetteer 97

Bibliography 131

FIGURES

Fig 1   The route of Crossrail constructions and buildings featured in
           this book 1

Fig 2   A Crossrail tunnel boring machine being lowered into position 2

Fig 3   London's population 1550-1901 5

Fig 4   The chronology of the development of aristocratic estates in the
           West End of London during the 17th–19th centuries 7

Fig 5   Ground floor plan of a typical small house in London after the
           great fire. Late 17th and early 18th-century 8

Fig 6   Cross-section of an early 19th-century estate house 8

Fig 7   Plan showing the location of buildings demolished ahead of the
           construction of the Crossrail station at Tottenham Court Road West 9

Fig 8   Plan of St Martins and St Giles Westminster, 1585, probably by
           Ralph Treswell 10

Fig 9   No. 101 Charing Cross Road (formerly No. 68 Crown Street) 11

Fig 10   Nos 67 and 68 Dean Street, a pair of Georgian terraced
           townhouses 11

Fig 11   Soho in 1746, detail showing Dean Street (Angel Hill) and Great
           Chapel Street, from John Rocque's Map of London, Westminster
           and Southwark of 1746 12

Fig 12   The west side of Soho Square, looking along Carlisle Street, from
           John Tallis's Street Views of 1838–40 12

Fig 13   Richard Horwood's map of 1792–9 showing the area of
           the Crossrail investigations between Dean Street and Great
           Chapel Street 13

Fig 14   No. 94 Dean Street in 2010 15

Fig 15   Vault beneath the road at No. 94 Dean Street in 2010 15

Fig 16   The ground floor of No. 94 Dean Street in 2009 15

Fig 17   Elevation drawing of the front of No. 94 Dean Street, 2009 16

Fig 18   First floor plan of No. 94 Dean Street, 2010 16

Fig 19   View of the first floor of No. 94 Dean Street 16

Fig 20   Partition at No. 94 Dean Street at second floor level 17

Fig 21   Staircase at No. 94 Dean Street at first floor level 17

Fig 22   Exterior view of No. 93 Dean Street in 2004 18

Fig 23   Exterior view of No. 9 Diadem Court in 2004 18

Fig 24   The timber staircase in No. 9 Diadem Court at ground floor level 19

Fig 25   Detail of a fireplace, west wall of the main first floor room of No. 9 Diadem Court 19

Fig 26   Detail of a fireplace in the north-west corner of the rear room on the second floor of No. 9 Diadem Court 19

Fig 27   View of fireplace in the west wall of the third floor main room at No. 9 Diadem Court 20

Fig 28   Detail of the staircase balusters, No. 5a Great Chapel Street 20

Fig 29   A hidden signature 'M' found on a rail of the staircase at No. 5a Great Chapel Street in 2010 21

Fig 30   Markets, river wharfs and industrial areas of London in the later medieval period 24

Fig 31   Cross-section of a representative building on Cheapside in the 17th-century showing both commercial and residential use 26

Fig 32   Plan showing the location of buildings demolished as part of Crossrail's over-site development of Tottenham Court Road Station East 27

Fig 33   The south side of Oxford Street, from Crown Street (later Charing Cross Road) to (Great) Chapel Street, from John Tallis's Street Views of 1838–40. 28-29

Fig 34   The businesses occupying the south side of Oxford Street, Nos 395–440, from John Tallis's Street Directory of 1840 30

Fig 35   Exterior view of No. 95 Dean Street in 2008 31

Fig 36   Exterior view of Nos 2–3 Fareham Street in 2010 34

Fig 37   Buildings demolished prior to the construction of Charing Cross Road in 1877–1887 35

Fig 38   No. 148 Charing Cross Road in 1892, with its distinctive pyramidal roof. To the right is No. 146 35

Fig 39   No. 148 Charing Cross Road in 2010 35

Fig 40   No. 148 Charing Cross Road: the spiral staircase at first floor level 36

Fig 41   No. 148 Charing Cross Road: detail of the coffered vaulted ceiling 36

Fig 42   The curved frontage of Nos 1–7 Oxford Street in 2009 36

Fig 43   No. 7 Oxford Street: fourth floor windows 37

Fig 44   No. 7 Oxford Street: original fireplace on the fourth floor 37

Fig 45   Nos 3 and 5 Oxford Street: Art Deco window surround in green marble 38

Fig 46   Nos 3 and 5 Oxford Street: Art Deco balustrade 39

Fig 47   Stanford's map of London of 1890 showing the areas granted to London's electric light supply companies 43

Fig 48   The electricity generating station at White Hart Depot, Plumstead, on 1:1250 OS map of 1957/8 44

Fig 49   View of White Hart Depot main building looking from North Road . . 44

Fig 50   View of White Hart Depot main building looking 44south-east 44

Fig 51   Willesden Electricity Power Station, Engine House, 1900. 45

Fig 52   White Hart Depot; internal view of the tiled former generating hall . . . 45

Fig 53   White Hart Depot: a) the excavated base of the brick chimney and
            of the concrete base of the cooling tower; b) detail of the central
            area of the chimney structure 46

Fig 54   Old Smithfield Market before closure in 1855 47

Fig 55   Smithfield Market in 2014 48

Fig 56   Smithfield Market in the late 19th century 49

Fig 57   Map showing the location of buildings demolished for . . . . the
            construction of the new Crossrail Farringdon Station east and west
            ticket halls 50

Fig 58   Smithfield Goods Depot in 1926; the lift is being used to move meat
            from the railway to the market 50

Fig 59   (a) No. 22 Long Lane; (b) No. 20 Long Lane 51

Fig 60   No. 3 Lindsey Street in 2009 51

Fig 61   A Plan of proposed alterations to the Great Western Railway depot
            at Smithfield in 1918 52

Fig 62   Nos 8–9 Hayne Street: a) the street frontage, b) detail of the rear of
            the building 53

Fig 63   Nos 22–23 Long Lane in use by Armour and Co., Chicago-based
            meat importers, prior to the building's conversion in the 1940s 53

Fig 64   The corner of the block at a) No. 2 Lindsey Street and b) No. 23
            Long Lane remodelled in Art Deco style 54

Fig 65   Nos 54–64 Charterhouse Street (Smithfield House) 54

Fig 66   Nos 54–64 Charterhouse Street (Smithfield House) rear view 54

Fig 67   The demolition of Nos 54–64 Charterhouse Street (Smithfield
            House) revealed the steel decking structure 55

Fig 68   Thames-side industries in the East End, from John Rocque's Map of
            London, Westminster and Southward of 1746 56

Fig 69   Plan showing the location of Crossrail works at the Albion Brewery,
            Whitechapel 57

Fig 70   Lined shaft of the artesian well revealed during excavations for
            Crossrail at the Albion Brewery, Whitechapel 58

Fig 71   Map of the countryside east of the River Lea in 1746 59

Fig 72   Stanford's Map of 1862 shows the building-up and industrialisation
            of East London 60

Fig 73   Plan showing the location of Crossrail at the former East London
            Soap Works 62

Fig 74   An advertisement for the East London Soap Works at Bow, 1862 62
Fig 75   An advertisement from 1904 for Lasso Soap, made at the East London
          Soap Works 62
Fig 76   The former East London Soap Works, Bow 63
Fig 77   The former East London Soap Works, Bow; interior of a factory
          building 63
Fig 78   25 Canada Square, Canary Wharf. Crossrail's offices 67
Fig 79   Bob Cratchit working by candle light at the offices of Scrooge
          and Marley 69
Fig 80   Plan showing the location of Nos 11–12 Blomfield Street 70
Fig 81   Nos 11–12 Blomfield Street in 2004 prior to demolition 70
Fig 82   Nos 11–12 Blomfield Street: geometric staircase 71
Fig 83   Nos 11–12 Blomfield Street: elaborate internal entrances 71
Fig 84   a) Nos 11–12 Blomfield Street: The hand crank for hydraulic lift
          found below the geometric staircase; b) A direct acting hydraulic lift . . . 71
Fig 85   The entrance to Nos 9–15 Oxford Street 72
Fig 86   Map showing the location of No. 2 Fisher Street 73
Fig 87   Ground floor plan of the sub-station and stores at No. 2 Fisher Street.
          Dec 1903 74
Fig 88   Fisher Street: elevation drawing from 1903 showing the Queen Anne
          style facade 75
Fig 89   Map showing the location of No. 65 Davies Street 75
Fig 90   Exterior view of No. 65 Davies Street 76
Fig 91   Caxton House 77
Fig 92   Cardinal House 77
Fig 93   Centre Point 77
Fig 94   The Remington Typewriter 78
Fig 95   W T Farthing's design for the replacement of The Green Man and
          French Horn on Dean Street in Soho 82
Fig 96   The Bath House as recorded in 2010 prior to its demolition 83
Fig 97   A variety of fonts greeted The Bath House's customers 83
Fig 98   Towards the end of the 19th century ground-floor arrangements
          in pubs started to change: a) The floor plan of The Green Man and
          French Horn in 1898; b) The floor plan of its 1899 replacement 84
Fig 99   An original cornice in The Bath House's club room 85
Fig 100   The final layout of The Bath House in 2010. The original partitions
          were long gone 85
Fig 101   The ornate carriage entrance between The Astoria and The Excelsior . . . 86
Fig 102   Map showing the location of The Barge in relation to Royal
          Victoria Dock in Canning Town 87

Fig 103   The Barge – formerly The Freemasons Tavern 2009 87

Fig 104   Details from The Freemasons Tavern's ornate entrance on
Freemasons Road 88

Fig 105   The corner of Charing Cross Road and Oxford Street. The Excelsior
is dwarfed by The Astoria 89

Fig 106   The Astoria in 2006 90

Fig 107   Crossrail's new Canary Wharf Station, May 2014 94

Fig 108   Crossrail's new Paddington Station: architect's impression 95

Fig 109   Crossrail's new Tottenham Court Road Station: architect's impression . . 96

ACKNOWLEDGEMENTS

Oxford Archaeology and Ramboll wish to thank Crossrail Ltd for commissioning this book, and Jay Carver, Crossrail's Lead Archaeologist, for assistance, commentary and guidance. We also wish to thank Jay's colleagues David Keeley, Marit Leenstra, Suzanna Pembroke and Iain Williamson. Our thanks also go to Treve Rosoman (Architectural Historian) who kindly read an earlier draft of this book and provided most helpful comments.

The authors have relied heavily on the survey reports that resulted from Crossrail's historic building recording programme. These surveys were undertaken by Oxford Archaeology/Ramboll, Museum of London Archaeology, Scott Wilson Ltd and Wessex Archaeology and we acknowledge the contribution made by the many members of staff from these organisations who took part in the surveys. Most survey reports have an acknowledgement section; these may be accessed at www.crossrail.co.uk. Most of the images reproduced in the present volume were prepared for the Crossrail surveys and are the copyright of Crossrail. The sources for all other images are given in the captions or (for re-drawn material) in the chapter end notes. Chapter 1 was written by Andy Shelley and Richard Brown, Chapter 5 by Richard Brown, Chapter 6 by Andy Shelley, and Chapter 7 by Ian Lindsay, Crossrail's Land and Property Director. Chapters 2, 3 and 4 contain the work of all the principal authors and contributors.

The surveys were commissioned by Crossrail Ltd or Transport for London and facilitated by Crossrail's or Transport for London's contractors. These included McGee (Tottenham Court Road west) and Laing O'Rourke (Custom House Station).

We gratefully acknowledge the assistance of our colleagues at Oxford Archaeology and Ramboll (Jacek Gruszczynski and Phil Emery).

We also wish to acknowledge the help we received from Qona Wright whilst sourcing information from the British Library, from Jeremy Smith for information from the London Metropolitan Archives and the staff at the Newham Archives and Local Studies Library. Amongst those who have helped us source or granted permission to use images we are grateful for the help of Karen Thomas and Andy Chopping from Museum of London Archaeology, Patrick Mannix from MOTCO, Nikki Braunton from Museum of London, Jovita Callueng from

The British Library, Emma Whinton–Brown from English Heritage, photographer Paul Talling, Sophia Brothers from the Science and Society Picture Library, Robert Leigh from Citigroup Realty Services, Matthew Llewellyn from Sectorlight, George P. Landow from The Victorian Web http://www.victorianweb.org, Matthew Lloyd from www.arthurlloyd.co.uk, Bob Lincoln from UK Power Networks, Ian Gunter from Numerical Science Ltd and special thanks to the editors of Grace's Guide to British Industrial History.

FOREWORD

Buildings define the identity of a city and provide a distinctive sense of place for its inhabitants and visitors alike. A major transport infrastructure project such as Crossrail is largely conducted beneath the streets of the city and is barely visible to the subterranean traveller. Its full impact is only revealed when they enter or leave on their journey. The new stations that are needed to serve this remarkable improvement to the communication network of central London have radically transformed the physical appearance of discrete areas of the capital and in the process have resulted in the demolition of a significant number of once-familiar buildings. Some of those buildings which have been sacrificed will be mourned by those who valued the delightful mixture of architectural styles and periods, particularly those on the fringes of Soho and along Oxford Street and the northern end of the Charing Cross road. Other demolitions, such as the faceless office blocks of the 1960s around the City will be welcomed. Whatever their intrinsic merits, they all have multiple stories to tell of those who lived and worked in them and of the ever-changing face of London over many centuries and that is what this book has set out to explore.

For those who like reading obituaries, there is a comprehensive gazetteer of each building that has been demolished along the line of the route, giving a brief summary of the known facts and illustrations of their former appearance and some of their details. They are all cross-referenced in the text which forms the bulk of the book and it is here that the record comes alive. Each chapter is given a theme to provide a broad context for the information on individual buildings which was revealed by the detailed research and recording that was carried out in advance of demolition. The result is a fascinating and engaging account of the domestic lives and occupations of ordinary Londoners living in the heart of the city. It is principally concerned with the Georgian and Victorian periods but it also touches on aspects of twentieth century life. The detailed contents of each chapter offer fresh insights on the adaptation of buildings to accommodate nineteenth century overcrowding and domestic occupations, the emergence of new industries and ways of working and, not least, opportunities for leisure and enjoyment away from the home.

New railways cannot be constructed either in crowded city centres or in tranquil rural landscapes without extensive change and destruction. The oxymoronic phrase 'preservation by record' can have a hollow ring but this study is an exemplary exception. It is a tribute to the responsible approach of Crossrail in commissioning appropriate mitigation, and equally to the professional investigators who have made such evocative connections between the individual buildings and the wider culture that they represent. The dissemination of their findings in this readable publication sets a high standard for future projects of this nature.

MALCOLM AIRS MA DPhil Oxford, FSA, IHBC, FRHistSoc

Malcolm Airs is the Emeritus Professor of Conservation and the Historic Environment, Oxford University Department for Continuing Education. He is a past President of the Institute of Historic Building Conservation, the Society of Architectural Historians of Great Britain and the Oxford Architectural and Historical Society. He has served as a Commissioner of the Royal Commission on the Historical Monuments of England and on the advisory committees of English Heritage and the Heritage Lottery Fund. He has been a member of both the Council and the Architecture Panel of the National Trust. He is currently a Trustee of the Landmark Trust and Oxford Preservation Trust.

CHAPTER 1

INTRODUCTION

There are three characteristics that most clearly define the aesthetic experience of a city: the layout of its streets, parks and gardens, the form of its buildings, and the infinite variety of people who use them. In London it is still possible to look around and be made aware of the historic evolution from field to metropolis. You may be standing in the City looking at the Roman wall, or at the Tower of London, or perhaps sitting on a bench in a Georgian square or a mirrored Victorian pub. The surroundings of your café in Canary Wharf will tell you much about London's 20th-century economic transformation.

For centuries London expanded radially, like a tree growing new rings. The establishment during the 1930s of the Metropolitan Green Belt

Fig 1 The route of Crossrail showing the location of the buildings featured in this book: (A) site locations in Greater London; (B) detail of Tottenham Court Road Station area; (C) detail of Smithfield Market area. Each building is identified by its gazetteer number

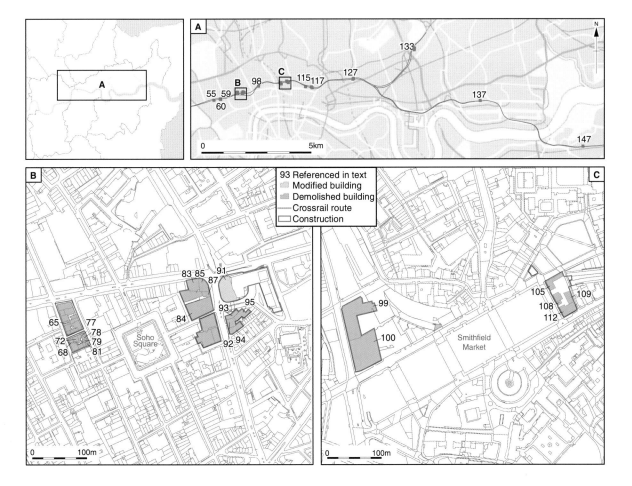

arrested this growth and as a consequece urban renewal intensified. As we write, Crossrail is threading across the city, linking east to west and opening another chapter in London's long history. The line (Fig 1) extends from Reading in the west to Shenfield and Abbey Wood in the east, with the new central London underground lines running from Paddington to Stratford north of the Thames and to Abbey Wood south of the Thames. New stations are being built at Paddington, Bond Street, Tottenham Court Road, Farringdon, Liverpool Street, Whitechapel, Canary Wharf, Custom House, Woolwich and Abbey Wood.

Crossrail is a project of enormous complexity and breathtaking magnitude. Much of it lies hidden below the city, visible only where new stations are emerging from the ground or tunnel entrances are being formed. At each of these worksites buildings have had to be adapted or removed. No building was touched before a process of enquiry and discussion with its owners and occupiers had taken place, and in each case the building was assessed and recorded by built heritage professionals. Buildings have much to tell us about the lives of others and historic buildings are, in the words of English Heritage (now Historic England), 'a living record of our social, economic and artistic history, as well as being powerful contributors to our sense of place and to feelings of local, regional and national identity'.[1] If removal of

Fig 2 A Crossrail tunnel boring machine being lowered into position

THE CHANGING FACE OF LONDON

a historic building is unavoidable, a record can mitigate the loss. In England, building recording generally conforms to one of four levels, ranging from a simple photographic record (Level 1) to a full historical and architectural analysis with accompanying photographs and drawings (Level 4).

Gathered together these records form an important corpus of information, but it is not one driven by any research agenda. Instead, they embody a wealth of little details and observations from which broad social themes and architectural developments may be teased. This book considers how the buildings examined in this way can tell us about the changing face of London. Each chapter takes as its starting point buildings that shared common relationships or characteristics. It reserves details for the gazetteer, which can be found at the end of this book. The gazetteer lists the relevant Crossrail reports for each building recorded, and these will be freely available through the Crossrail website.[2]

It is hoped the book is received as it is intended: a celebration of buildings that individually may have passed unremarked but collectively added to the common wealth. It is also a snapshot of the moment when Crossrail's promised stimulus to urban renewal and growth becomes a reality.

NOTES

1 English Heritage 2006, 2
2 www.crossrail.co.uk

CHAPTER 2

DOMESTIC LONDON

London's changing demography

The story of London's architectural development has to be viewed against the backdrop of the city's relentlessly rising population (Fig 3) and the continual expansion of the occupied area on both sides of the River Thames as the largest city in England during the 19th century became the largest in Europe and then the largest in the world.

Fig 3 London's population (red line) grew steadily from the 1550s to the Great Plague of London in 1665, when 100,000 Londoners died. After the plague London's population initially recovered but then started to flatline and then very slightly decrease. In the late 18th century London's population began to increase again steadily. From 1801 to 1901 London's population increased dramatically from 818,129 in 1801 to 3,585,323 in 1901.[1]

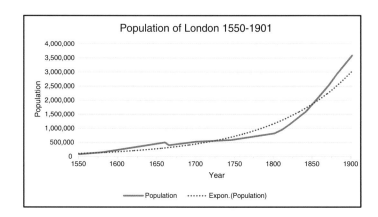

London's vitality has always depended on incomers: by the end of the 18th century Georgian London was a city of migrant workers. Most of the migrants had moved from elsewhere in England, Scotland, Wales and Ireland, but around 2% of the population were of foreign origin, including 25,000-40,000 French Huguenots, 5,000-10,000 African, Caribbean and Asian people and 15,000-20,000 Jews. Foreign migrants who arrived without wealth tended to settle in the East End of London, whereas the craft workers and the wealthy moved to the West End. The impact of the migrant population on the architecture of London can be seen in church buildings, which served the local ethnic communities around them.[2]

Urban growth always creates a tension between internal expansion crowded into existing settlement and the drive to expand and move out. The City of London was bursting out of its medieval walls by the mid 16th century, and had grown mainly westwards. Its depiction in the Civitates Orbis Terrarum (Atlas of Cities of the World) published by Georg Braun and Frans Hogenburg in 1572 shows the urban landscape as it was at the accession of Queen

Elizabeth I in 1558. Smithfield market was located on the west edge of London, but the city had begun to expand along Holborn and along the Strand down to Westminster. By 1720 when John Strype's survey of London appeared, the city had developed to the east and north but a greater extent of the development was westwards and Smithfield was in the centre of the city. From the mid 16th century to 1690, a period of only 140 years, London's population increased fivefold from approximately 80,000 in 1550 to nearly half a million.[3]

The 18th century saw the development of the West End of London as a residential quarter. By the late 18th century a hierarchy of wealth became evident was apparent in many areas of the city, as people began to be separated by class in a complex social geography where not only the East End/West End divide was evident. In all areas the social circles in which a person moved was dictated by their address.[4] In the Victorian era these distinctions became more evident pronounced as the gap between the rich and poor increased in the centre of London. The separation of home from place of work had begun in the 18th century, but accelerated in the 19th century as the provision of public transport enabled people to move to the suburbs and live away from their work. Population growth and better transport links facilitated a massive expansion of the metropolis in physical as well as population terms, and it paved the way for the world-class city that we know today.[5]

The Georgian housing boom

The growth of Stuart and Georgian London was characterised by the ordered development of the larger west London estates. The aristocratic owners of peripheral urban farmland built a series of squares linked by a hierarchy of greater and lesser streets that created a new urban form. The first experiment with this new form based on Italian influences was Inigo Jones's Covent Garden piazza, laid out for the Duke of Bedford in 1631. This was followed in the 1650s by Lincoln's Inn Fields, and continued after the Restoration with the development of Bloomsbury Square and St James's Square in the 1660s, and Soho from the 1670s. Development accelerated from the middle of the 18th century onwards. The development of aristocratic estates in the West End of London from the 17th century to the mid 19th century can be mapped (Fig 4).[6]

Covent Garden introduced a new style of architecture based on the classical principles of proportion, restraint and regularity, with the individual houses built in brick and stone and set in long and uniform terraces. The house plan that was developed for the new classically inspired terraces was simple and standardised: one room at the back and one at the front on each floor, with a passage and staircase at one side (Figs 5 and 6).[7]

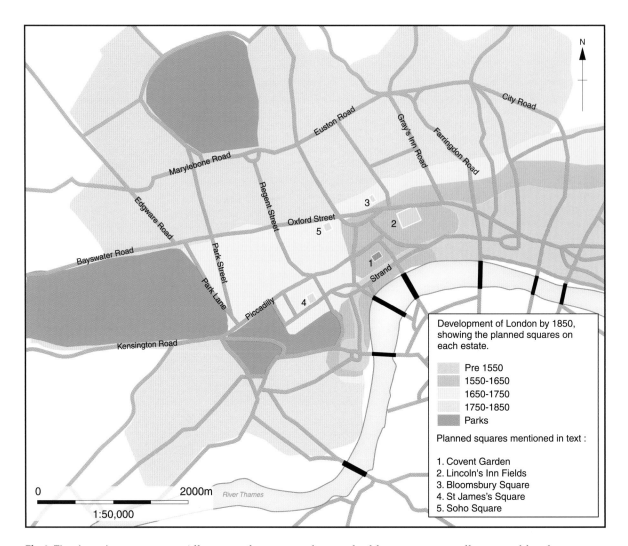

Development of London by 1850, showing the planned squares on each estate.

Pre 1550
1550-1650
1650-1750
1750-1850
Parks

Planned squares mentioned in text :

1. Covent Garden
2. Lincoln's Inn Fields
3. Bloomsbury Square
4. St James's Square
5. Soho Square

Fig 4 The chronology of the development of aristocratic estates in the West End of London

All except the poorest houses had basements, usually created by the combined effect of a shallow cut below ground level and a build-up of the road in front. Basement storage often extended into fuel stores that ran beneath the pavement as far as the kerb of the road. The houses usually extended over three or four storeys from ground level, with attics in the roof space. Well-off families could afford to use each floor for a different purpose. The lower floors were used for the kitchens and for eating, the middle floors for receiving guests and sleeping and the upper floor for servants. The reception rooms, where guests were entertained, were the most lavishly appointed, and family rooms were also well decorated, but the servants' rooms at the top of the house were plain.[8] Particularly on the side streets away from the more prestigious squares, lower floor space was often used for shops, workshops or the business premises of professionals, with living accommodation above.

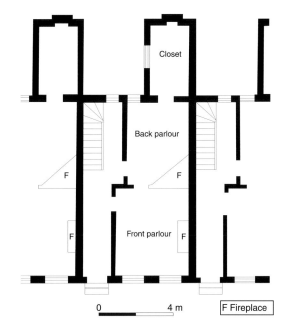

Closet

Back parlour

F

F

Front parlour

F

F

0   4 m

F Fireplace

Fig 5 Ground floor plan of a typical small house in London after the Great Fire

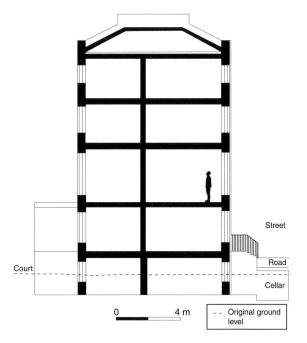

Street

Road

Cellar

Court

0   4 m

- - - Original ground level

Fig 6 Cross-section of an early 19th-century estate house, showing the ground level built up on both the street side and the court behind. The cellar was below the road, which allowed coal to be emptied down a shute into this space.

Victorian London

Throughout the Victorian period London continued to grow both in population and in area. By the later 19th century the old inner districts were increasingly given over to commerce, manufacturing and entertainment and their associated infrastructure. Only the very richest and the poorest lived in the centre; the rich because they could still afford to live grandly, the poor because they could not afford to move anywhere better. The middle classes and the better-off working classes were gradually migrating outwards, a process greatly facilitated by the introduction of horse-drawn omnibus services from 1829, which enabled tradesmen and clerks to move into the inner suburbs and commute to work. From the 1840s the railways intensified these trends, by enabling the middle classes to commute from further afield, while the building of railway lines led to the destruction of the homes of more than 100,000 people in central London and the inner suburbs, which greatly increased central overcrowding. From the late 1860s horse trams and cheap rail fares enabled the better-off working classes to commute from the East End suburbs. The physical landscape around London was dramatically altered by the end of the 19th century, as the growing city swallowed up former villages in Middlesex, Surrey, Essex and Kent.[9]

Crossrail in Soho

Crossrail's extended and upgraded Tottenham Court Road Station west is located at the north-west corner of Soho, at the junction of Oxford Street with Dean Street and Great Chapel Street. The development of the new station required the demolition of several blocks of buildings in the area, which are shown on Figure 7. Many of these only dated back to the

Fig 7 Buildings demolished ahead of the construction of the western ticket hall at Crossrail's Tottenham Court Road Station. Buildings discussed in the text are shown in blue and labelled with their gazetteer numbers

Reproduced from Ordnance Survey digital map data © Crown copyright 2015. Supplied by Crossrail Ltd. under PMSA

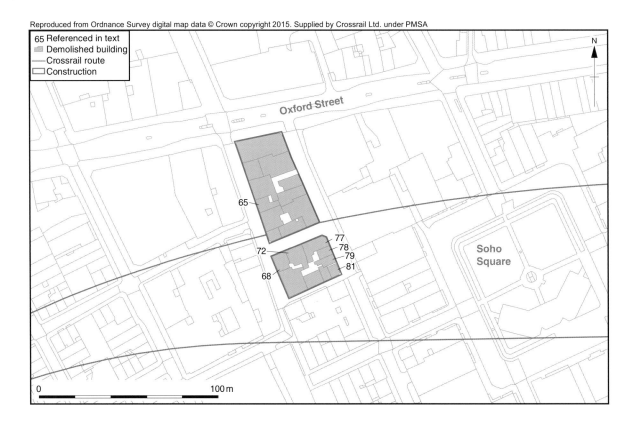

THE CHANGING FACE OF LONDON

Present day Oxford Street

Fig 8 Plan of St Martins and St Giles Westminster, 1585, probably by Ralph Treswell (The National Archives, MPB 1/1)

rebuilding of the area after Second World War bomb damage, but a number were identified as retaining older fabric and features of historical interest, and were recorded by Crossrail before they were demolished. These buildings provide us with an unusual insight into the changing fortunes of a famous district of London, which mirror the wider developments discussed above.

Until the middle of the 17th century, the area that was to become Soho was still open countryside. The earliest detailed view we have is a plan probably drawn by the celebrated London surveyor Ralph Treswell in 1585 (Fig 8). Oxford Street ('The Way from Uxbridge to London') runs across the top of the plan towards the village of St Giles in the Fields. Soho would develop a hundred years later across the area of the large field to the south and west, which Treswell labels 'The fielde called St Gilles fielde'. The later Wardour Street, Hog Lane (later Crown Street, and replaced eventually by Charing Cross Road) and Shaftesbury Avenue followed the lines of the lanes Treswell shows running around the outside of St Giles Field to the west, east and south respectively.

For over a century, as the pressure for housing grew, the government tried to control building around the periphery of London, particularly

Fig 9 No. 101 Charing Cross Road (formerly No. 68 Crown Street) is one of only a handful of early houses to have survived the construction of Charing Cross Road in the late 19th century

unauthorised construction of cottages by the poor. In 1670 Sir Christopher Wren petitioned the king for a new proclamation against the building 'in Dog Fields, Windmill Fields, and the Fields adjoyning to So Hoe' of 'small and meane habitations' which it was feared would enable the poor and the offensive trades, to colonise the area. Instead, licences were soon being granted to aristocratic landowners for the development of new estates.[10]

In 1677, Richard Frith, citizen and bricklayer, who was heavily involved in numerous development projects in the West End, obtained the lease of 19 acres of Soho Fields together with a royal licence to build. Frith and his partners soon ran into financial difficulties, but it seems that most of the streets and houses, including Soho Square, had been built by about 1691. The remaining area, chiefly the north-west end of Dean Street and the courts on its western side, was built up in the 1690s. By 1721 there were around 715 occupied houses.[11] The only major changes to the late 17th-century street plan of Soho have taken place on the very edge of the area, with the creation of Charing Cross Road and Shaftesbury Avenue in the 1880s. Although many of the buildings have been much altered and reconstructed, the street plan and the narrow house plots date from the original laying out of the estate in the late 17th century, and still give the area a special character.[12] The Grade II listed No. 101 Charing Cross Road (Fig 9) is a rare example of a late 17th to early 18th century terraced house in London. Its survival is remarkable as it was originally on Crown Street, which was almost completely redeveloped when Charing Cross Road was constructed. Other early survivals are Nos 67-68 Dean Street (Fig 10), which date from 1731-3.[13]

The freehold of most of Soho Fields was granted to the Earls (later the Dukes) of Portland in 1698 by the Crown and remained in their hands for much of the 18th century. There is evidence to suggest that some of the late 17th-century building had been of a poor quality, and it is clear that there was a substantial phase of rebuilding associated with the new leases granted by the Duke of Portland from the late 1720s onwards. The north-western part of the Soho Fields estate seems to have seen much rebuilding from around 1734 onwards, particularly in Dean Street, Diadem Court and much of Great Chapel Street, with a new cross-street, Titchfield (later Fareham) Street, constructed at this time between Great Chapel Street and Dean Street.[14] The street plan of the area shown by John Rocque in 1746 (Fig 11) is recognisably that of the present day.

Fig 10 Nos 67 and 68 Dean Street, a pair of Georgian terraced townhouses

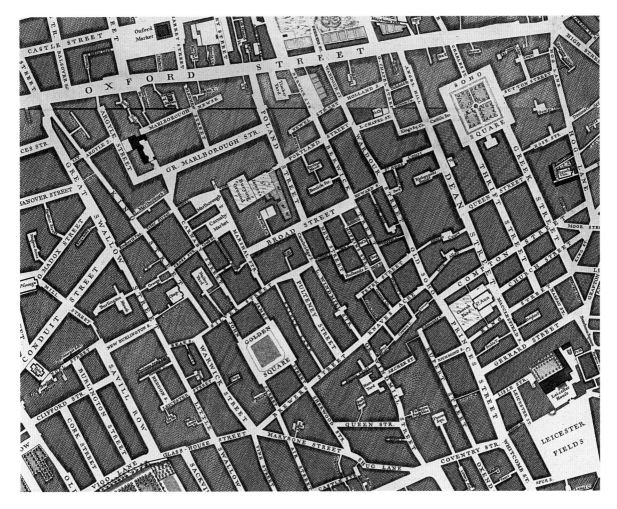

The most prestigious houses were located in Soho Square and the streets that led from it. Some streets, including the middle part of Dean Street, contained large houses for the well-to-do, but many houses in Soho were smaller. These were often only two windows wide, and the standard of building was lower than elsewhere in the West End.[15] By the early 18th century the character of Soho was already starting to change, with the grander inhabitants abandoning the area in favour of the more exclusive and better built new estates being developed to the north and west. In their place came foreign communities, particularly French Huguenot refugees, professional and trades people, and artists (Fig 12).

By the 1790s, the Portlands were in financial difficulties and were preparing to sell the estate. A detailed survey was drawn up in 1792-3, which shows a mixture of rebuilding of the 1720s and 1730s on original late 17th-century fabric, with further rebuilding evident particularly in the southern part of the estate in the late 18th century. The 1792-3 survey shows that the plots on the Portland estate were mostly 18-20 feet wide and 70-80 feet deep.

Fig 11 Soho in 1746, detail showing Dean Street (Angel Hill) and Great Chapel Street, from John Rocque's Map of London, Westminster and Southwark of 1746 (MOTCO)

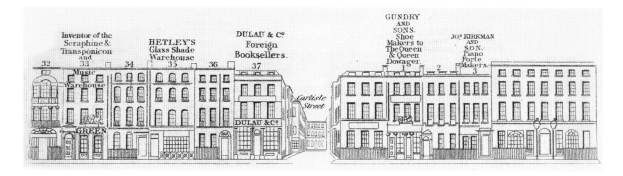

Fig 12 The west side of Soho Square, looking along Carlisle Street, from John Tallis's Street Views of 1838-40 (Museum of London)

The houses, mostly built in mirrored pairs, are two rooms deep, extending back about 30–35 feet from the street, with a closet wing at the back, and a yard behind. By the time of the survey, many of the yards contained cottages or workshops often let on a separate tenancy. Most of the shops were located around Compton Street, but a few were starting to appear elsewhere, and many of the houses were being used for professional trading purposes or as small manufactories, as well as dwellings.[16]

Richard Horwood's map of London of 1792-9 (Fig 13) shows the area in great detail. The site of Crossrail's Tottenham Court Road western ticket hall occupies two islands of small buildings between Dean Street and Great Chapel Street, separated by two cross-streets, Titchfield (later Fareham) Street and Crown (later Diadem) Court.

Fig 13 Richard Horwood's map of 1792-9; detail showing the area of Crossrail's site between Dean Street and Great Chapel Street (MOTCO)

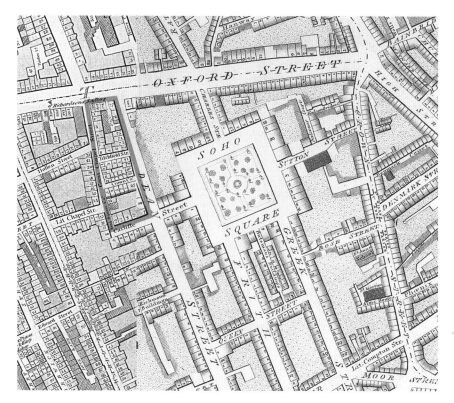

THE CHANGING FACE OF LONDON

The break-up of the Portland estate meant that ownership of property in Soho became very dispersed, with much less regulation of building and occupancy. By the middle of the 19th century Dean Street's inhabitants included doctors and private teachers, craftsmen such as bakers, shoemakers, leatherworkers, piano-makers and graphic artists, small manufacturers, tailors and a chiropodist. By 1900 there were fewer professionals and small craftsmen in the street, and more manufacturers, workshops and restaurants.[17] By the late 19th century, however, Soho was also experiencing severe overcrowding. The appalling conditions in which some of the inhabitants were living were described by Arthur Sherwell, a Liberal politician, temperance campaigner and social reformer:

. . . one case (in Soho) was reported to me of a working man with a wife and a large family, who had barely enough sleeping accommodation for themselves, but who nevertheless, took in several bakers as lodgers. The lodgers were away all night, and came home to sleep in the daytime, so that in this way the beds were always occupied. Precisely the same thing happened in another house in the same district. The announcement that may sometimes be seen in Soho of "Part of a room to let", represents what is frequently a very serious aggravation of the evils of overcrowding. In one case a small back-room was occupied by a young, newly-married couple, who took in a single-man lodger who slept in a chair-bedstead. In the same house two back-rooms, both small, were occupied by a man and his wife and three men-lodgers, and the rooms were further let out at night for gambling purposes at the rate of one shilling per hour. Subsequently the woman (whose husband was a baker and therefore away all night) got rid of the men-lodgers and boarded a prostitute, and let her rooms out to this woman as a common brothel.

In a neighbouring street a small back-room was occupied by seven persons, viz., a family consisting of a man, his wife, and three children; and two (sometimes three) lodgers. A tenant in the same house gave information that part of the occupants stayed up gambling (which was always being carried on) while the others slept; but even then it seemed probable that some must sleep under the bed as well as upon it.

A house in another street of which information was given me was fearfully over-crowded. In two rooms were a family of eleven persons, viz., a man, his wife, and nine children (one a son 20 years of age, a daughter 19, another 14, another 13, and several below this age), and a lodger aged 22, making twelve persons in all. The man was a tailor and carried on his trade in the same room. They slept four in a bed.[18]

NO. 94 DEAN ST

A block of houses towards the north end of Dean Street were recorded by Crossrail (Nos 93–5). Of these, No. 94 was considered to be the best

Fig 14 No. 94 Dean Street in 2010 (Scott Wilson Ltd)

preserved (Gazetteer No. 79). It can be seen on Horwood's map of 1792, where it is labelled No. 69. It was listed by Historic England in 1978 as an early 18th-century four-storey terraced house, two windows wide, that had been re-fronted in Stock brick in the mid 19th century, with a shop front on the ground floor dating from the same period (Fig 14).

In January 2009, when the first recording work took place for Crossrail, the ground floor and basement were occupied by the Pompidou Coffee Shop, with domestic accommodation on the floors above. It is likely that this kind of mixed use had a long history here, as elsewhere, and may have been the pattern of occupation since the 18th century. In 1808 the building was occupied by T. Dawes, Cabinet maker and Upholsterer, and in 1818 by Dawes & Newton Cabinet Makers and Upholsterers[19] and subsequent directories list a boot and shoe maker, a cobbler, a painter and a stationer.

The Crossrail investigations have provided important new information about the history of the building. Rather than being an 18th-century house, it is likely that it had in fact been largely reconstructed in the early to mid 19th century. The only earlier elements were probably the two vaulted basement storerooms that had been built out under the road (Fig 15).

However, the building's modest external appearance would still have been very much in keeping with the style of the area. In its final form No. 94 had a flat roof with a roof terrace, but this is likely to have been a later 20th-century alteration, and the 19th-century house probably had a pitched roof with attics.

Fig 15 Vault beneath the road at No. 94 Dean Street in 2010, looking east

Fig 16 The ground floor of No. 94 Dean Street in 2009, looking east

At street and basement level the original fabric had been much altered to form large open rooms for food preparation and service (Fig 16). Above this level, however, the three residential floors preserved the original layout of the building, each with a larger principal room at the front and a smaller back room overlooking the yard behind. The principal rooms each had a pair of mid 19th-century sash windows over-looking Dean St (Fig 17), while the back rooms had a single sash window of the same date. Surviving panelling beneath the front windows was of Victorian type. Each room had originally been provided with a fireplace in the north wall, but in every case these had subsequently been removed and only the hearth bases survived below later replacement floorboards. The residential floors were reached by a staircase in the south-west corner of the house, accessed by a separate doorway and passage from Dean St (Fig 18).

When the house was vacated prior to demolition it was possible to investigate its fabric more closely (Figs 19 and 20). The evidence for extensive rebuilding came from the upper floors as the 19th-century east-west joists between the first and second floors had been morticed and nailed into an older central north-to-south beam between the main rooms. This beam had been re-used from an earlier building, perhaps the earlier house on this site. On each floor the two rooms had been divided by a stud partition, also in places the partitions retained marks of the original lath and plaster construction, which had been replaced with modern plasterboard.

Fig 17 Elevation drawing of the front of No. 94 Dean Street, 2009 (Scott Wilson Ltd)

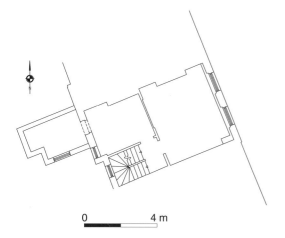

Fig 18 First floor plan of No. 94 Dean Street, 2010

Fig 19 View of the first floor of No. 94 Dean Street, looking east towards the street

Fig 20 (left) Partition at No. 94 Dean Street at second floor level, looking west towards the rear of the property

Fig 21 (right) Staircase at No. 94 Dean Street at first floor level, facing south

The stair in the south-west corner of the house was one of the most interesting internal features. The newels, balusters and finials were of Georgian style, possibly dating to around 1734 (Fig 21). However, close investigation of the stairs prior to their removal showed that the treads, risers and joists were not of Georgian construction, while the handrails and decorative elements were all slightly different. It seems most likely that the stairs were rebuilt along with the rest of the house in the 19th century, but re-used older elements, some of which might have survived from the original Georgian house on the site. The final flight of stairs, leading from the third floor to the roof terrace, was much plainer and would originally have given access to servants' rooms in the attic.

In the mid and late 19th century the house was often occupied by several different families and the census records reveal a high turnover of inhabitants. In 1851 the occupants comprised three households totalling 15 individuals. The three households were Henry Bird, a house decorator, with his wife Catherine and their six children, Richard Cox, a jeweller, with his wife Rebecca a 'pearl stringer', three children and a servant, and Thomas Pryer, a cabinet turner. Ten years later only one family is recorded, that of Elizabeth Barritt, widow and tobacconist, who was living here with four children and a servant. The family seems to have been relatively well-off; the two sons were both recorded as engineers, and the adult daughter was a milliner, while the second daughter was still at school. By 1871, however, the house was home to 19 people in eight different households. There was Alfred Dawson, a French bookseller, together with his French wife and their son Alfred; John Brown, a chairmaker from Cornwall, with his wife and son; William Rolfe, a tailor from Poland; Lagarde Antoine, a tailor from France with his wife Amelie and their son Leon; Francis Ovella, an Italian liquor maker with his wife Harriet; Abigail King, dressmaker; James Rodwell, a labourer, with his 13-year-old son Henry who was an errand boy; and Sophia Chapman, who was a dressmaker from Essex, with her three children. In 1891 Lorenza Abba, an Italian restaurant keeper, was here with his French wife Adolphine, a French cook Raymona Cosson, and an Italian waiter, Beniamino Fraser. Ten years later the property was divided between seven separate households with 12 people, of whom 11 were born in Italy. The occupants included four hotel waiters, three hotel cooks, a housemaid, a commercial traveller and a solicitor ('feeble minded').[20] Although No. 94 probably offered two rooms on each of s ix floors (if the basement and attics are included) some of the late 19th-century households can hardly have been occupying more than two rooms at most, and some only one.

The front of No. 94 was tied into the front of No. 95 to the north (see Chapter 3 Fig 35), implying that both had been reconstructed at the same time. Although the parapet heights of the two buildings were the same, the ornate ground floor shop front of No. 95 and the windows on the upper floors, were all set higher than their plainer counterparts in No. 94, and there was no attempt to emulate the modest uniformity of a Georgian facade. As a result, No. 95 had a much more assertive street presence, and its history (see Chapter 3) reflects greater stability and prosperity.

Fig 22 Exterior view of No. 93 Dean Street in 2004

NO. 93 DEAN STREET

No. 93 Dean Street (Gazetteer No. 81), to the south of Nos 95 and 94, occupied a corner plot with frontages onto both Dean Street and Diadem Court (Fig 22). The four-storey building recorded as part of the Crossrail project was constructed of London Stock brick probably in the mid 19th century on the site of an earlier corner building, the plot being shown on Horwood's map as No. 68 (see Fig 13).

In 1841 the building was the occupied business premises of John Ferguson, an engraver and printer. He also lived on the premises with his wife Jane, young daughter Marion, and an older relative, probably John's mother, also called Marion. In addition to the Fergusons, there were nine other people living in the house in 1841. There was a young female servant, Mary Foley, probably working for the Fergusons. John Cocking, a stationer, Louise Smith, a servant, and Ellen Bath a young girl aged 5, formed another household, and a third household comprised Robert Norman, a tailor, and Ann Norman, and Lucy Williamson and Mary Harsant, two young women of independent means, together with a young girl aged 4 years also called Mary Harsant.

In 1851 there were 24 people in three households occupying the property. There was George Gissing, unmarried, a bootmaker, with eight lodgers including a family of five. All the lodgers were working in the boot and shoe making trade, except for the younger son of the family, who was an errand boy. The second household comprised John Pope, a brewer's workman, and his wife, and George Cole, a painter and his wife Georgina and their three children who lodged with them. The third household comprised John Lynch, a tailor, his wife Mary and their six children. By 1861 No. 93 was home to at least 23 people, comprising six families and two single tenants, both of whom were Irish and described as 'Charing woman'. There was Thomas and Hannah Miller and their two daughters; Elizabeth Yarnold, dress maker and her two children; a newspaper reporter and his wife; two tailors with their families; and a couple born in Paris.

Ten years later Jane Boyce, a 54-year-old dressmaker, was living here with her dressmaker daughter and five lodgers, one of whom, Harriet Allen, was from Rye and of independent means. The other lodgers were four Germans, one of whom, August Hahn, is described as a Professor of Chemistry. By 1881 the building was occupied by two households. The first comprised Ambrose Jacobs, a grocer, his wife and five children and a lodger William Beck, a bootmaker. The second household consisted of Jane Boyce and her daughter with three lodgers.[21]

Fig 23 Exterior view of No. 9 Diadem Court in 2004

Fig 24 The timber staircase in No. 9 Diadem Court at ground floor level, facing north

NO. 9 DIADEM COURT

No. 9 Diadem Court (Gazetteer No. 80) immediately to the west was of very similar build to No. 93 Dean Street and may have been contemporary,

Fig 25 The fireplace, in the main first floor room of No. 9 Diadem Court

Fig 26 The fireplace in the north-west corner of the rear room on the second floor of No. 9 Diadem Court

THE CHANGING FACE OF LONDON

as the two buildings shared a continuous moulded red brick cornice (Fig 23). The freeholds were offered for sale together in an advertisement in The Standard in February 1900. At the time of the advertisement both buildings were let on lease and produced 'the very low rent of £105, rising shortly to £110 and later to £115 per annum'.

A number of Victorian fittings survived at No. 9, including a staircase in the north-east corner with turned timber newel posts, stick balusters and a moulded handrail (Fig 24). Parts of the original Victorian skirting and dado rail were still attached to the walls around the staircase, and a number of original cast iron fireplaces survived on the first floor (front room), second floor (back room) and third floor (both front and back rooms) (Figs 25–27).[22]

NO. 5A GREAT CHAPEL STREET

No. 5a Great Chapel Street (Gazetteer No. 65) was a late 19th-century four-storey building with a shop front at street level and three floors above, each with three sash windows fronting the street. In 1895 it was used by a dealer in building materials, and hatches for lifting and lowering goods had been set into each floor towards the south-west corner. Despite its apparently recent age, the building unexpectedly contained an in situ historic staircase, which had a half-turn with winders form and extended from ground floor up to third floor level. It had square section newel posts with a square cap and turned balusters to the main flights (Fig 28), and is datable to the 1730s. It seems very likely that the late 19th-century building

Fig 28 Detail of the staircase balusters, No. 5a Great Chapel Street

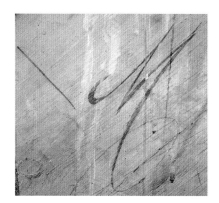

Fig 29 A hidden signature 'M' found on a rail of the staircase at No. 5a Great Chapel Street in 2010, possibly the carpenter's signature

had been reconstructed around this staircase. Removal of a covering board revealed the letter 'M' with elaborate curled flourishes written on the uppermost side rail. This structural rail would have been hidden behind a facing board and would almost certainly never have been visible to the occupants of the house, so it is quite possible that this is the initial of the original carpenter, who left his signature here (Fig 29).

London's population increased by a factor of five between the mid 16th century and the end of the 17th century. This was an incease which imposed a terrible pressure on the city's housing stock. The demand was met in part by continued increasing of the housing density, and sub-division of properties and in part by expanding the limits of the city, particularly to the west. Expansion here was fuelled by the development of the larger west London estates, planned areas marked by a deliberate separation between social classes. An even more dramatic period of population growth occurred in the Victorian period, and the inevitable pressure on the housing stock that followed was exacerbated by the emergence of large-scale and land-hungry industries and transport networks. Overcrowding was the inevitable result.

Inspecting the capital's surviving pre-20th century housing stock is an excellent way of understanding how demographic changes such as these were accommodated. Noting where changes have occurred in a building, and identifying if possible when those changes happened, are critical aids in this process. This chapter has attempted to draw lessons from the historic dwellings inspected during the course of Crossrail's construction. Inevitably, it has more to say about the domestic architecture of the relatively well-to-do than it has about the housing endured by the poor, for the simple reason that the houses of the middle classes have survived whereas those of the poor have not. Even when records demonstrate that the latter were formerly severely overcrowded, the evidence for the desperate conditions that must have prevailed amongst the poor has been largely swept away. Where buildings had remained residences, 20th-century improvements had removed evidence of poorer conditions, and where buildings had changed use the new uses had the same effect. In the next chapter, some of the evidence for commercial use or re-use of such buildings is examined.

NOTES

1   Sources used for population information: (**1550, 80,000**) People in Place, Families, households and housing in London 1550-1720, The Institute of Historical Research

(2003-2008), http://www.history.ac.uk/cmh/pip/pip.html [accessed 15 August 2014]; (**1580, 150,000; 1660, 500,000**) Ross and Clark 2008, 84; (**1665, 400,000**) Forsyth 2008b, 110; (1700, 527,000) Old Bailey Online, Emsley, Hitchcock and Shoemaker, A Population History of London, The Demography of Urban Growth, 1674-1715, http://www.oldbaileyonline.org/static/Population-history-of-london.jsp [accessed: 07 April 2014]; (**1745, 586, 750**) Locating London's Past, 2011, Version 1.0, Population Statistics and Notes (Downloads), Bills of Mortality, 1740s, London Population Estimates, 1690s, 1740s, 1800s (Excel with Notes and additional worksheets) http://www.locatinglondon.org/static/Population.html#toc4 [accessed: 07 April 2014]; (**1801-1901**) 'Table of population, 1801-1901', A History of the County of Middlesex: Volume 2: General; Ashford, East Bedfont with Hatton, Feltham, Hampton with Hampton Wick, Hanworth, Laleham, Littleton ed. William Page (London, 1911), pp. 112-120. http://www.british-history.ac.uk/vch/middx/vol2/pp112-120 [accessed 12 March 2014]

2 Old Bailey Online, Emsley, Hitchcock and Shoemaker, Community Histories: Huguenot and French London. http://www.oldbaileyonline.org/static/Huguenot.jsp: accessed 20 September 2014; Ross, 2008c, 134-135

3 Barker and Jackson 1990, 12-13, 50-1; for population figures see Note 1

4 see Porter 1994, 93-5

5 Werner 2008c, 212-213

6 For Covent Garden, Summerson 1945, 14-16; Fig 4 after Barker and Jackson 1990, 12-13, 26, 50-51, 117

7 Summerson 1945, 34, 50; Figs 5 and 6 after ibid., figs 5 and 7 and English Heritage 1996, 3, 16 and Fig 1

8 Ross, 2008b, 126-127

9 Porter 1994, 225-7, 231

10 'General Introduction', in Survey of London: Volumes 33 and 34, St Anne Soho, ed. F H W Sheppard (London, 1966), pp. 1-19 http://www.british-history.ac.uk/survey-london/vols33-4/pp1-19 [accessed 11 August 2014].

11 'The Development of Soho Fields', in Survey of London: Volumes 33 and 34, St Anne Soho, ed. F H W Sheppard (London, 1966), pp. 27-36 http://www.british-history.ac.uk/survey-london/vols33-4/pp27-36 [accessed 23 September 2014].

12 City of Westminster, *Conservation Area Audit: Soho & Chinatown*, 8-12

13 'The Pitt Estate in Dean Street: Nos. 67 and 68 Dean Street', *Survey of London: volumes 33 and 34: St Anne Soho* (1966), pp. 210-212. http://www.british-history.ac.uk/survey-london/vols33-4/pp128-141 [accessed: 16 May 2014]

14 'The Development of Soho Fields', in *Survey of London: Volumes 33 and 34, St Anne Soho*, ed. F H W Sheppard (London, 1966), pp. 27-36 http://www.british-history.ac.uk/survey-london/vols33-4/pp27-36 [accessed 23 September 2014].

15 City of Westminster, *Conservation Area Audit: Soho & Chinatown*, 9

16 'The Portland Estate in Soho Fields', in Survey of London: Volumes 33 and 34, St Anne Soho, ed. F H W Sheppard (London, 1966), pp. 37-41 http://www.british-history.ac.uk/survey-london/vols33-4/pp37-41 [accessed 23 September 2014].

17 'Dean Street Area: Portland Estate, Dean Street', in Survey of London: Volumes 33 and 34, St Anne Soho, ed. F H W Sheppard (London, 1966), pp. 128-141 http://www.british-history.ac.uk/survey-london/vols33-4/pp210-121 [accessed 23 September 2014].

18 Sherwell 1901, 35-6

19 *Post-Office Annual Directory for 1808 . . . of London and Parts Adjacent*, London, p 79; *Johnstone's London Commercial Guide and Street Directory*, London 1818, p 159.

20 Censuses of England and Wales 1851, 1861, 1871, 1891, and 1901

21 Censuses of England and Wales 1841, 1851, 1861, 1871, and 1891

22 Window ironmongery, architrave and skirting samples, together with staircase sections, both from the Tottenham Court Road buildings and houses in Dean Street were recovered by the Brooking Collection together with neo-classical doors, circa 1922, from the Astoria cinema in Charing Cross Road. At the time of writing these pieces are in store. For up-to-date information on The Brooking National Collection, please see the website: www.thebrookingcollection.org

CHAPTER 3

COMMERCIAL LONDON

Introduction

Like all medieval towns, London was a centre of craftworking and marketing, but during the later medieval period it took an ever-increasing share of the country's trade. The main markets were located between Cheapside and the river, with the exception of the cattle market at Smithfield outside the city to the west. The wharfs and quays stretched from the River Fleet to the Tower (Fig 30)[1]. In the present chapter we look at evidence for shops and small businesses. The next chapter discusses larger-scale operations associated with the mass production of food, brewing, electricity and soap making.

By 1700 London handled 80% of the nation's imports, 69% of its exports and 86% of its re-exports. Vast quantities of food and fuel were brought from the surrounding regions to feed the growing population. The most significant change in this period was the reorientation of international trade away from Europe towards the Americas, Africa, India and the East Indies. By 1700, a third of England's imports came from Asia and America, and many of them were then re-exported via London to continental Europe. A marked feature of this period is the growing power of mercantile joint-stock trading companies enjoying monopolies conferred by royal charter. The most successful of these was the East India Company, which monopolised trade with the Far East for over 200 years.[2]

The financing of trade became ever more sophisticated as markets expanded and both the risks and the profits increased. The city's medieval trade had long made it the most powerful financial centre in the kingdom, but the expansion of trade in the later 16th and 17th centuries, and the growing power of English merchants, created a need for new resources on an increasing scale. The Royal Exchange, opened in 1570, became the principal public meeting place for merchants and traders. During the 17th century London's goldsmiths operated as private bankers, taking money on deposit and lending at interest. Goldsmith bankers provided an effective private banking system for London, and many developed into long-lasting private banking firms such as Coutts & Co.

The Bank of England was founded in 1694 to raise a war loan for the Government and to manage its finances; it also undertook commercial business. In 1734 it moved to its present site at Threadneedle Street,

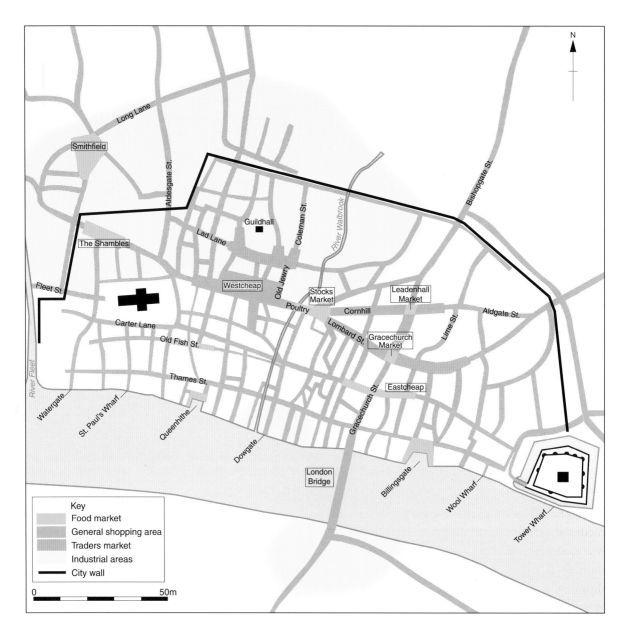

Key
Food market
General shopping area
Traders market
Industrial areas
City wall

0   50m

Fig 30 Markets, river wharfs and industrial areas of London *c* 1320. After Barker, F & Jackson P, 1990, 12-13; Bradley & Pevsner, 1997, 44, 48, 413-626, Ekwall, 1951, 81-87, Harben, 1918, Porter, 1994, 27, and Ross 2008a, 78, 81

opposite the Royal Exchange, and the coffee houses and taverns of the area became a centre for the burgeoning trade in money, insurance, stocks and shares and, perhaps just as importantly, information. Famously, the 'coffee-house' seating arrangement was to become a permanent feature of the Lloyds of London insurance offices until the 20th century. The terms of the Bank of England's Royal Charter effectively restricted the development of other large banks in England, although there were numerous private banks run by wealthy individuals such as goldsmiths and industrialists. The former were found exclusively in London and the latter developed in the provinces over the course of the 18th century. It was not until the 19th century that restrictions were lifted to allow the development of new joint-stock banks.[3]

By the late Victorian era, the City's banks had become a global financial power and purpose-built banks began to appear with offices above to accommodate the clerks needed to write letters and fill the ledgers. The architecture of the larger banks tried to imitate the grandeur of the Bank of England, giving an impression of high status, solidity and financial security. The modern system of branch banking was begun by the larger banks in the mid 19th century, with one central bank in the City acting as a headquarters for subsidiary branch banks operating in urban centres outside London. Branch banking was made possible in the later 19th century and improved in the 20th century through technological developments, including the telegraph and telephone, the rail and road networks and the development of cheques. Over the course of this period, as the commercial pressures on small banks increased, they were forced to close or merged into the larger banks in order to survive.[4]

The medieval open markets remained a centre of commerce in London until the late Georgian period, and purpose-built shopping streets initially grew up around the markets. In 1666 the Great Fire of London destroyed 80% of the buildings in the city, most of which were made of timber. This has meant that it is difficult to study commercial buildings before the late 17th century except from excavated remains and documentary sources. A few early commercial buildings do survive, like the 17th-century Grade II* listed Nos 41-42 Cloth Fair, which is likely to have been a cloth shop conveniently located between Bartholomew Fair and Smithfield Market.

The purchase of goods in bulk was undertaken at fairs or markets, and medieval shops were probably much smaller than shops of later periods. Many, like the 'selds'[5] around the centre of London, may have been no more than lock-up stalls sharing larger premises. Until the 18th century shops were usually found on the ground floor of multi-purpose buildings, as seen, for example, in 17th-century properties on Cheapside and All Hallows Honey Lane, and indeed many small shop premises have continued to be located on the ground floor of multi-purpose buildings right up to our own time (Fig 31). Key changes to affect small shops include the development of window glazing, and the realisation that shops, originally open stalls closed by shutters, could have permanent glazed display fronts. Small Georgian glazing units were ideal for mixing visibility with security, while the gradual development of larger and stronger sheets of rolled or floated glass by the mid 19th century allowed shop windows to become larger and their displays more elaborate.

Shops and markets followed the expansion of London westwards, and during the 18th century 'high-class' shops appeared in the City, Piccadilly

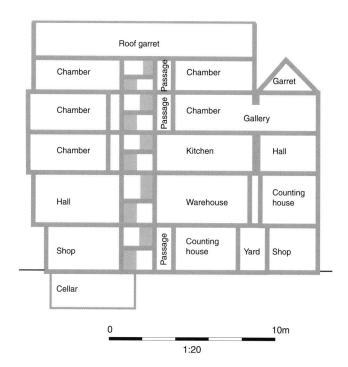

Fig 31 Cross-section of a representative building on Cheapside in the 17th-century showing both commercial and residential use. Many timber structures of this date were arranged back to back with interconnecting passages to adjacent buildings and overhanging jetties. This partly explains why the Great Fire of 1666 spread so rapidly between properties.

and Mayfair. By the early 19th century London's celebrated shops ran from Whitechapel through the City and along the Strand to Charing Cross, and from Shoreditch along Cheapside to Holborn, St Giles and Oxford Street, with the later Victorian addition of Knightsbridge and Westbourne Grove. A Victorian development was the department store, with the earliest being established by William Whiteley in Westbourne Grove. Large stores also developed around Tottenham Court Road. Oxford Street became a centre for drapery and women's fashion accessories and Bond Street specialised in men's tailoring.[6]

Crossrail and commercial London

The construction of Crossrail has provided opportunities to record a range of buildings connected to London's commercial and industrial past. Perhaps some of these buildings would have seemed very ordinary to the casual observer, but each is a product of its time and has something to tell us about London's recent history and the way in which the streets and buildings of London reflect the wider developments discussed above.

The development of Crossrail's new Tottenham Court Road Station entailed the demolition of six blocks of buildings. Two blocks in Soho lay south of Oxford Street between Great Chapel Street and Dean Street and separated by Fareham Street (see Fig 7). The third and fourth blocks (Fig 32) stood on the west side of Charing Cross Road at its junction with Oxford Street. The fifth and sixth blocks were located on the east side of

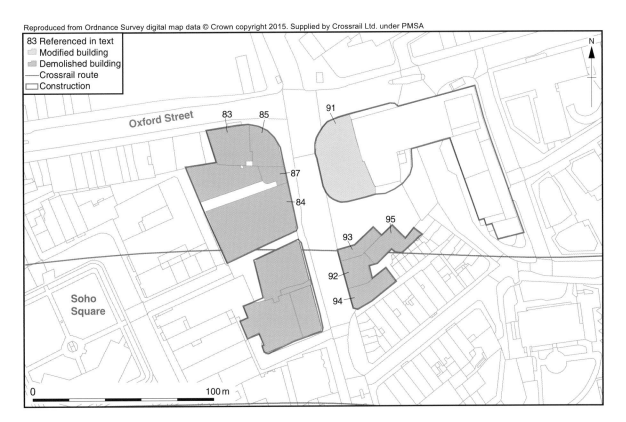

83 Referenced in text
Modified building
Demolished building
—Crossrail route
Construction

Oxford Street

Soho Square

0   100 m

Charing Cross Road between New Oxford Street and Denmark Place. These were separated by Andrew Borde Street (named for the last Master of St Giles's Hospital, which stood near here).

Oxford Street and Soho

Oxford Street has long been one of the principal access routes into London from the west. During the 18th century its character was transformed by the development of major residential estates along its length to north and south, and general improvements undertaken by the turnpike and paving commissions. By the 1780s it had become a fashionable shopping street, but the small-scale family business still predominated, based in buildings that provided shop space at the street front and domestic accommodation behind and above. In 1786 a foreign visitor, Sophie von La Roche described '... *a street taking half an hour to cover from end to end, with double rows of brightly shining lamps, in the middle of which stands an equally long row of beautifully lacquered coaches, and on either side of these there is room for two coaches to pass one another; and the pavement, inlaid with flag-stones, can stand six people deep and allows one to gaze at the splendidly lit shop fronts in comfort . . . Up to eleven o'clock at night there are as many people along this street as at Frankfurt during the fair, not to mention the eternal stream of coaches. The arrangement of the shops in*

Fig 32 Plan showing the location of buildings demolished as part of Crossrail's oversite development of the eastern ticket hall for Tottenham Court Road Station. Buildings discussed in the text are shown in blue and labelled with their gazetteer numbers

Fig 33 The south side of
Oxford Street, from Crown
Street (later Charing Cross
Road) to (Great) Chapel
Street, from John Tallis's
Street Views of 1838-40
(Museum of London)

*good perspective, with their adjoining living-rooms, makes a very pleasant sight. For
right through the excellently illuminated shop one can see many a charming family
scene enacted: some are still at work, others drinking tea, a third party is entertaining
a friendly visitor; in a fourth parents are joking and playing with their children*[7]

Some 50 years later, in his Street Views of 1838-40, John Tallis shows us the
south side of Oxford Street, from Crown Street (later Charing Cross
Road) to (Great) Chapel Street (Fig 33). The street is lined with 'modest,
irregular Georgian houses with shop fronts'[8] and Tallis lists the wide
variety of small businesses operating there (Fig 34). No shops of this date
survived within the area of Soho investigated by Crossrail, but there were
examples of similar types of buildings that had been extensively refurbished
or rebuilt in the 19th century.

NO. 95 DEAN STREET AND ITS OCCUPANTS

No. 95 Dean Street (Gazetteer No. 78), along with the adjacent No. 94 (see
Chapter 2) had probably been extensively rebuilt in the mid 19th century
on the ground plan of earlier buildings. Unlike its plainer neighbour to the
south, however, No. 95 had an eye-catching facade with decorative upper
floor window surrounds and a Victorian shopfront framed by plain pilasters
and console bracketed capitals each with a flower boss.

In 1841 there were 13 people in No. 95 Dean Street probably forming
three households. No. 95 was the business premises of George Leake,
who was a scale maker, and he and his wife Susannah, and their four
children George, David, Henry and Frances lived on the premises. Also in

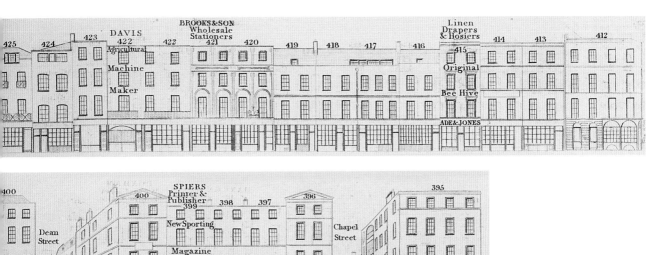

the household were William Stuart (20 yrs), probably Susannah's relative, and Amelie Handley (15 yrs) a female servant. George Leake had married Susannah Stuart at St George, Bloomsbury on 23rd June 1829. George had been born in Middlesex, but his wife Susannah was from Exeter in Devon.

John Scott, a watchmaker, his wife Martha, and their son James also lived at No. 95 in 1841. The third household consisted of Mary Genesis, a pew opener, and her son James Haig (15 yrs) a messenger. In 1851 Mary Ann Genesis (59 yrs), pew opener and her son James Heigg (28 yrs) together with a lodger James Hoisey lived at No. 422 Oxford Street.

Although George Leake was still listed as trading from No. 95 in the *Post Office London Directory* for 1850, at the time of the 1851 census he and his wife Susannah were living at No. 6 West Street, Soho, and No. 95 was occupied by Kyrle Ward carver and gilder and his family (see below).[9]

In 1851 No. 95 was occupied by 17 people, forming four households. All the heads of households were involved in the carving and gilding trades. Kyrle Ward, his wife Jane, two children Eliza (12 yrs) and Thomas (2 yrs) and servant Bridget Coleman (18 yrs) formed one household. Jane was Kyrle Ward's second wife, Eliza was his youngest daughter from his first marriage and Thomas was his son from his second marriage. Kyrle Ward had been born in Ireland *c* 1790–1800 and his first wife was Mehetabel Shipley, whom he had had married at St George Bloomsbury on 30th June 1824. The couple had had five children. In 1841 Kyrle and Mehetabel Ward had lived at Tudor Place, St Pancras. Mehetabel died in the mid 1840s and Kyrle

TALLIS'S STREET DIRECTORY.

OXFORD STREET, DIVISION I.

1	Edridge's Candle and Oil Warehouse.	399	Spiers, Printer and Publisher.
2	Combs' Wine Vaults.	400	Fitchew, Silversmith.
3	Tate and Haines, Cheesemongers.	☞	Dean Street.
4	Parkin, Confectioner.	400	Rippin's Wine Vaults.
5	Layfield, Grocer.	401	Edghill, Tailor.
6	Boar and Castle Inn and Hotel.	402	Spiers, Shoe Maker.
7	Whiskin's Patent Medicine Warehouse.	403	Conibeere and Co. Drapers.
8	Riddle, Coachmaker.	404	Miller, Bookseller.
9	Turner's China and Glass Warehouse.	405	Kleyser and Co. Clock Makers.
10	Bell and Argill, Auctioneers, &c.	406	Bridges, Turner, &c. to her Majesty.
11	Williamson and Draper, (Star Brewhouse.)		Davis, Ham and Beef Shop.
12	Vigo, C. Salesman.	407	Bramble, Watch Maker.
13	Drake's Feather Bed Warehouse.	408	Balls and Son, Music Sellers.
14	Thornton's Coffee House.	408½	Bonham, Water Closet Maker to Her Majesty
15	Painter and Co. Feather Bed Warehouse.	408	Wyatt, Tobacconist.
16	Watson, Stove Grate Manufacturer.	409	Smith, Hosier.
17	Hutchins, Butcher.	410	Foster's Auction Rooms.
18	Vialls, Dyer.	411	Hancox, Tailor.
19	Davies, Outfitting Warehouse.		Crape, Wine Merchant.
20	Towns and Co. Music Warehouse.	☞	Charles Street.
21	Thursfield, Oilman.	412	Shepherd, Baker.
☞	Hanway Street.	413	Eryan, Boot Maker.
22	Lewis, R. Silversmith.	414	Cranch, Wine Vaults.
23	Taylor's Carpet Warehouse.	415	Ade and Jones, Linen Drapers.
24	Moore, W. and E. Undertakers.	416	Barras, Tobacconist.
☞	Rathbone Place.	417	Harwood, Saddler.
24	Wright, J. Grocer	418	Baronto, Alabaster Warehouse.
25	Foster and Co. Linen Drapers.	419	Field, T. Auctioneer.
26	Odling, Surgeon, &c.	420	Bishop's Dairy.
27	Robinson's Picture Warehouse.	421	Brooks, Wholesale Stationer.
28	Tavener and Kimpton, Linen Drapers.	422	Beard, Tailor.
29	Maltwood, Trunk Maker.	422 a	Davis, Machine Maker.
28	Bennett and Turrell, Bonnet Warehouse.	423	Harding, Basket Maker.
29	Honeywill and Co. Coach Makers.	424	Pike, J. Baker.
29	Wilson and Co. Wine Merchants.	425	Kearns, Cutler.
☞	Perry's Place.	426	Churcher, Corn Dealer.
30	Livermore and Son, Ironmongers.	427	Cole, Hosier.
31	Grant's Fancy Warehouse.		Jessop's Toy Warehouse.
32	Barlow, Writing Desk and Case Warehouse.	428	Jefferys, Window Blind Manufactory.
33, 34	Munn's Furniture Warehouse.	429	Sneezum's Wine Vaults.
36	Applegath's Bonnet Warehouse.	430	Aiken and Co. Upholsterers.
37, 38	JACKSON and GRAHAM, House Decora-	431	Austin, Rope and Twine Maker.
	tors, &c. (See Vignette.)	432	Askew's Bird Warehouse.
39	Treherne's Furniture Warehouse.	433	Bonsor, Candle and Soap Manufacturer.
☞	Newman Street.	434	Bailes, Bedstead Maker, &c.
40	Perry, Watch Maker.	435	Dean, Surgeon.
395	Barnes, Coach Maker.	436	Brown, Chemist, &c.
☞	Chapel Street.	437	Hutchinson's Dining Rooms.
396	Fairlam's Wine Vaults.	458	Bowman, Tobacconist.
397	Valentine, Tinman.	459	Glasscock, Baker.
398	Nosetti, Carver and Gilder	440	Webb, Cheesemonger.
399	Minnifie, Hair Dresser.		

FROM THE LINCOLN GAZETTE.—One of the wonders of the present age, and not the least too, is a most singular and successful effort, to depict a plan of London, and we believe that other towns are to follow, by giving a representation of each street, with the front of every house. It is a most amusing and useful affair: besides endless variety of architectural effect displayed in contrast, the several inscriptions and sign-boards are faithfully recorded, and the work serves for a directory, as well as a street plan, which will enable a stranger to recognize the identical house in any street to which he may wish to proceed. The street views appear in numbers, each containing upwards of one hundred buildings, shewing both sides of the street, elegantly engraved on steel, and is accompanied by a clever historical description of the locality. It is a fund of entertainment and is executed in a style that renders it worthy of a place on the drawing room table. Now, at what rate per number is such a novelty charged? Two shillings? No—one shilling? No—sixpence? No. Our readers will be amazed to learn that the faithful outline representation of any street in London, with its shops, churches, public buildings, &c., and a beautiful view of some prominent edifice, a neat plan of the locality, and historical discription, are supplied at the wonderfully cheap rate of three-half-pence!

Fig 34 The businesses occupying the south side of Oxford Street, Nos 395–440, from John Tallis's Street Directory of 1840 (Museum of London)

Ward married Jane Morisey at St Leonard Shoreditch on 6th April 1848. Jane's father Thomas Morisey was a shoemaker.[10]

Jane Ward must have died soon after the 1851 census was taken, because Kyrle Ward remarried on 8th August 1853. His third wife was Mary Rebecca Carpenter, the daughter of a jeweller. According to the parish register Kyrle Ward was 51 years old and Mary just 30. Kyrle Ward died in late 1855 and his will was proved on 2nd January 1856. He seems to have been moderately prosperous and bequeathed Mary 'all of my stock in trade, furniture, fixtures, plate, linen, books, china, pictures and every article and thing I be possessed of.'[11]

Also living at No. 95 in 1851 were Bernard W Holmes, a gilder, and his wife Susanna, and children James, Mary Jane and Richard. In 1861 Bernard and Susanna Holmes and their five children were living in Little Titchfield Street, Marylebone. The third household comprised William Child, another gilder, and his wife Elizabeth. William Child was born in Shrewsbury and his wife Elizabeth was from Bath. The fourth household was George Clark, a carver, who was a widower, and his married sister-in-law Ann Clark, and George Clark's children Alexander and Ellen, and his father John Clark, a chair maker.

By 1861, however, No. 95 Dean Street was occupied by a single household comprising William James Court (born Oxford 1806), his wife, two visitors and a servant, Mary McLean from Ireland. Like Kyrle Ward, William Court (50 yrs) was a gilder and his wife was Ward's widow Mary, whom Court had married on 5th October 1856. Their visitors in 1861 were Mary Carpenter (14 yrs) and Thomas Ward (12 yrs). Mary Carpenter must have been a relative, perhaps a niece, of Mary Court (née Carpenter), and Thomas Ward was the son of Kyrle Ward and his second wife Jane Morisey and therefore Mary's stepson. Mary Rebecca Ward was probably William Court's second wife. She died in 1866 and was buried at All Souls cemetery, Kensal Green on 28th May 1866; she was just 43 years old.[12]

Fig 35 Exterior view of No. 95 Dean Street in 2008 (Crossrail)

William Court then married Catherine Augusta Kemble in 1868. Catherine was the daughter of Thomas Kemble, shoemaker, and was just 24 years old. William and Catherine Court together with a single female servant were the sole occupants of No. 95 in 1871 and 1881. William Court died on 30th March 1882, and left a personal estate valued at £339 15s. The probate register describes him as a 'dealer in Gilders' materials'. Presumably No. 95 had been his place of business. Catherine remarried on 29th October 1883 at St George Bloomsbury. Her new husband was Josephus Guillielmus De Martelaere, merchant of No. 95 Hart Street, Bloomsbury, and son of the late Jean Baptiste De Martelaere cloth manufacturer.[13]

In 1889 Joseph was letting out rooms for rent at No. 95 Dean St. A notice appeared in The Era newspaper dated 13 April, in the name of J Guillaume, advertising furnished apartments near all theatres, 'French and Belgian spoken. Piano, if wanted', while a month later the apartments, with 'moderate charges', were advertised with the inducement 'On Parle Francais et Flamand'. In the 1891 census, however, No. 95 Dean Street was occupied by a single household comprising a police constable James Brittan (born Fermanagh, Ireland), his wife Rachel, who was a caretaker, and their son Charles (12 yrs).

In 1901 No. 95 was occupied by two households. The first household was James William Turner, (colour) oilman and shopkeeper, and his wife Eliza Harriet Turner. The second household comprised Jesse Pittard, packer and furniture dealer, his wife Mary and daughter Annie, who was a 'relief stamper'. Jesse Pittard (58 yrs) was from Somerset, and his wife from Steyning, Sussex.

James Turner died aged 51 in 1910, but Eliza continued to trade from the premises, and was still there in 1911, when she was registered along with a visitor, Daisy Dormer (25 yrs) an assistant lampshade maker. There was a second household at the address in 1911 comprising Jean van Gils, stonemason (53 yrs) and his wife Maria Matta, a linen maid in a hotel (46 yrs). Jean van Gils was from the Netherlands and his wife Maria was from Brussels, Belgium. They had been married 24 years.[14]

NO. 93 DEAN STREET

The domestic occupation of No. 93 Dean Street (Gazetteer No. 81) has been discussed in Chapter 2. The building had a ground floor shop, with display windows on both its Dean Street and Diadem Court frontages (Fig 22). The chamfered corner created an additional fifth bay. The building was not recorded internally, but there were three doors from the street, and these give some clues about how the access to the building worked. The doorway on Diadem Court was plain and positioned beyond the end of the shopfront; it presumably gave access to stairs leading to domestic accommodation on the upper floors, and was possibly later a separate entrance for lodgers. The northernmost door on Dean Street was original, and was more decorative, being recessed with a fluted surround; this may have been the access into the shop originally, but a later shop door had been inserted into the frontage immediately to the south and the north door may have been a private entrance for the main tenant. The Post Office and Kelly's Directories show that this building was occupied by a variety of businesses and shops over time, including in 1841 John Ferguson, an engraver and painter, who also lived on the premises with his family (see Chapter 2). In 1871, the only occupants were Mrs Jane Boyce a dressmaker, her daughter and five lodgers. These were four German men and a woman of independent means from Kent. The access arrangements suggest this may have been a more substantial boarding house business. In 1881 Jane Boyce was still living in the building with her daughter and three lodgers, but Ambrose Jacob and his family also lived at No. 93, and Ambrose Jacob ran a chandler's shop on the premises as recorded in the 1882 *Post Office London Directory*. In 1900 the building was occupied by Benjamin Mark, a tailor, and in 1915 Andrea Cicomi, a confectioner, had his business in the building. In 1950 it was occupied by Jack Carruthers's Café and by the

1960s there was a celebrated French Coffee bar called *Les Enfants Terribles* in the basement. *The Black Gardenia* nightclub opened there in 2007.

NO. 9 GREAT CHAPEL STREET/NO. 4 FAREHAM STREET

No. 9 Great Chapel Street, another late 19th-century building on a corner plot, had one facade on Great Chapel Street and the other on Fareham Street (Gazetteer No. 68). It was very much of its period and constructed of red brick in builder's 'Norman Shaw'[15] style with typical decorative features including three horizontal white stone string courses, decorative friezes on the second floor, a moulded stone cornice with brick parapet above and embellished brick gables on the third floor. The original main entrance is likely to have been in the centre of the Great Chapel Street frontage where there was a doorway with a fanlight, pilasters and an arched pediment. The building also had a shop frontage with display windows that extended along the whole of its Fareham Street frontage and up to the doorway on the Great Chapel Street side. The directories show that the building was used as a laundry in 1900, a bicycle manufacturers in 1915 and in 1950 a film producers, but the architecture would suggest that domestic use was intended on the upper floors.

LIGHT INDUSTRIES

In the 19th century the districts of Soho, St Giles and the Strand were home to a multitude of workshops and domestic manufacturing units. In 1897 around 30% of the workers were employed in tailoring, shoemaking, shirt making and dressmaking, and these occupations occur regularly in the census lists of those living in Nos 93-95 Dean Street, along with carvers, gilders, furniture makers, book sellers and wax chandlers.

While some of the traditional employments survived, by the late 19th century, despite its proximity to Oxford Street, Soho was very much in decline as a residential area. The social reformer Arthur Sherwell considered that one of the chief causes of the decline was the 'enormous' displacement of residential dwellings by warehouses and shops:

. . . it is certain that the displacement of dwelling-houses by business premises very considerably aggravates the problem of overcrowding in industrial districts. The increased value of land as sites for business premises, and the consequent constant decrease in the number of dwelling-houses, leads to a corresponding increase in rents. The more prosperous classes migrate to other districts, while the poor, who must be near their work, remain, and become more and more crowded. It is this process that has sent up rents in London 150 per cent, in fifty years, and made Soho, as I shall presently show, one of the most densely crowded districts in London.[16]

Fig 36 Exterior view of Nos 2-3 Fareham Street in 2010

Two of the buildings recorded for Crossrail in this area represent exactly the process Sherwell describes. No. 5a Great Chapel Street (Chapter 2, above) had been rebuilt on the site of a Georgian house to form the premises of a builder's merchant; the existence of hatches for lifting goods on all floors of the building suggests that it no longer contained residential accommodation. Nos 2-3 Fareham Street (Fig 36; Gazetteer No. 72) formed another late 19th- or early 20th-century purpose-built workshop, albeit with some pretensions to style. The facade on Fareham Street contained the main entrance and two large arched openings (probably originally vehicular entrances) in 'rusticated' brickwork with horizontal bands and string courses. The three upper floors each had identical rows of three arched windows, which originally lit large single rooms until partitioned in the 20th century. The building was used as a manufacturing unit from 1900 or earlier and until at least the 1950s. William Betteridge & Co, jewel case makers, are noted as using the building in 1900 and 1915. By 1925 it was listed simply as manufacturers and by 1950 had two occupants, F Sale & Co., packing manufacturers, and S Sinitsky, a working tailor.

OXFORD STREET AND CHARING CROSS ROAD

Until the late 19th century the boundary between the east side of Soho and the adjacent parish of St Giles in the Fields was formed by Crown and Castle Streets. The idea of providing better connections from the new railway stations of the West End had been discussed for many years, but it seems to have been the opening of Charing Cross Station in 1864 that eventually brought matters to a head, and the Metropolitan Board of Works obtained the necessary powers to build Charing Cross Road in 1877. The route of the proposed new road followed the existing Crown and Castle Streets closely on the west side, but the buildings on the east were to be entirely demolished to create a much wider thoroughfare (Fig 37). Additionally, the buildings on the corner of Oxford Street and Crown Street were to be demolished to allow the junction to be widened. Land acquired by the Board that was not required for the new road was to be leased for new building. Charing Cross Road was opened in February 1887 and the new leases were put out for tender.

A number of the buildings constructed after the opening of the new road were recorded by Crossrail. On the east side of Charing Cross Road Nos 138-146 (Gazetteer Nos 92-4) formed a short row that had survived the construction of Centre Point (see Chapter 5). Nos 142 and 146, and No. 148, were designed in 1888 and are recorded in a photograph of 1892 (Fig 38).

Nos 138-40 appear as a single building on the Ordnance Survey plan of 1894 and were occupied in 1895 by Alderman, Johnson and Co., who

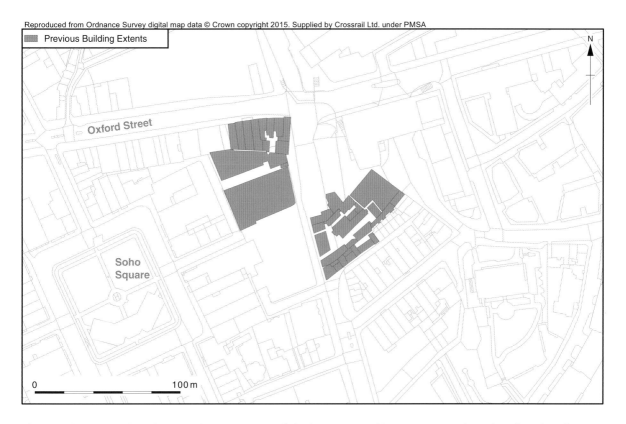

Fig 37 Buildings demolished prior to the construction of Charing Cross Road in 1877-1887 are shown in red, against the background of a later street plan

Fig 38 (left) No. 148 Charing Cross Road in 1892, with its distinctive pyramidal roof. To the right is No. 146 (English Heritage Archives, BL 11863)

Fig 39 (right) No. 148 Charing Cross Road in 2010

COMMERCIAL LONDON

manufactured invalid carriages, couches, chairs and perambulators; by 1915 this was the premises of Francis Day and Hunter, one of the many firms of music publishers in the area. Nos 142 and 146 were two separate properties within a single symmetrical building. At the front were two shops separated by a central port-cochère giving access to No. 144 in the yard behind known as Crown Place. The latter was the premises of G W Scott and Sons, basket manufacturers in the late 19th and early 20th century, and the letters SC visible in the 1892 photograph (Fig 38) above the passageway are probably part of their sign. The photographic apparatus manufacturer Jonathan Fallowfield, whose shop sign appears in the 1892 photograph, occupied No. 146 and was there until 1923.

No. 148 Charing Cross Road was a particularly distinctive building designed by Bateman and Bateman of Birmingham, with a large inset arch dominating the facade on the first and second storeys. The third floor had three windows with stucco surrounds scored to resemble ashlar, and the building was covered by a tiled pavilion roof. The 1892 photograph shows a display of lighting in the first floor window, likely to be that of James Hinks and Son, a brasswork and lighting manufacturer. From 1915 until the 1960s Walsh, Holmes and Co., music sellers, were here.

Inside the building was a large room, which spanned the first and second floors, and had a stage, a wooden spiral staircase (Fig 40), and a coffered vaulted ceiling (Fig 41) to the third floor. When the building was occupied by a nightclub it was known as the Ballroom. Previously it had been used as a music rehearsal space.

Fig 40 No. 148 Charing Cross Road: the spiral staircase at first floor level

Fig 41 No. 148 Charing Cross Road: detail of the coffered vaulted ceiling

Fig 42 The curved frontage of Nos 1-7 Oxford Street in 2009

Nos 1–7 Oxford Street (Gazetteer No. 85) stood on a key site on the corner of Oxford Street and Charing Cross Road (Fig 42). The older corner buildings had been demolished for the creation of Charing Cross Road's widened junction with Oxford Street, and the replacement buildings that were recorded by Crossrail were built as a single phase. They formed a curved red brick terrace of commercial buildings with classical detailing, divided into four separate premises, Nos 1, 3, 5 and 7 Oxford Street. No. 7 was the least altered and retained its original fire surrounds, staircase and balusters, door and window architraves, and other fittings (Fig 43).

Fig 43a No. 7 Oxford Street: fourth floor windows

During the 1930s, the two central buildings (Nos 3 and 5) were joined to become a branch of Barclays Bank and completely refaced to give a distinctive unified front dressed with Portland stone. The bank front incorporated elements of classical design and would have been expensive to build as the decoration was hand-carved. The stylish effect was carried into the interior, where Art Deco features had been used. Window surrounds of green marble (Fig 44a) survived on the first floor, along with coffered plaster ceilings on the ground floor and a staircase with elaborate iron balustrades and fluted panelling in the stairwell (Fig 44b).

In contrast to Barclays confidently adorned facade, AMRO Bank, the occupants of No. 101 Moorgate, are likely to have been entirely content with the simple glass and concrete clad exterior that their new London headquarters offered when it opened in 1981 (Gazetteer No. 115; Fig 45).

Fig 43b No. 7 Oxford Street: original fireplace on the fourth floor

Fig 44a (left) Nos 3 and 5 Oxford Street: Art Deco window surround in green marble on the first floor

Fig 44b (right) Nos 3 and 5 Oxford Street: Art Deco balustrade

Fig 45 101 Moorgate, London office of AMRO Bank

The speculative office development offered restaurant and retail space at ground floor level, reserving the upper floors for AMRO and thus keeping the bank's employees away from contact with the general public. A private atrium, complete with ornamental pool, emphasised this exclusive arrangement. The building had a short life; AMRO (by then ABN AMRO) found itself at the centre of the financial crisis of 2007–2010, by which time in any case the building was scheduled to make way for Crossrail's new Liverpool Street Station western ticket hall.

The modern day prevalence of multi-storey, steel-framed office buildings has its roots in the technical innovations of Paxton's Crystal Palace of 1851 where the concept of the iron (later steel) supporting frame was proven. The modernist architectural movement argued that form should follow function but undoubtedly for many developments the basic nature of the steel frame and 'curtain wall' or 'hung cladding' construction means that financial considerations are the driving force. In addition, such buildings very easily lend themselves to open-plan office working.

Although built almost a decade apart, there is little to distinguish the frontages of No. 18 Hanover Square (designed in the early 1960s by architectural practice Ronald Fielding Partnerships) and its neighbour No. 19 Hanover Square (built in 1973) (Gazetteer Nos 59–60; Fig 46). Both were six storeys high (with basements) and clad with glass and concrete panels. Number 18 was described by the architectural historian Nikolaus Pevsner as 'rather elegant but far too bulky to suit the character of the square'. Both were demolished to make way for the Crossrail's Bond Street Station eastern ticket hall.

From this chapter we can see how the details to be found in many of London's buildings are clues about their commercial past. For example, some of the basic characteristics of the shop, a building-type that emerged from the market stalls of medieval London, were observed in a number of buildings recorded by Crossrail. In the crowded capital of a country that the French revolutionary Bertrand Barère de Vieuzac had described as a 'nation of shopkeepers', the Victorian shopfront emerged. Eye-catching and highly decorative, plots such as No. 93 Dean Street and No. 9 Great Chapel Street were especially highly prized because they presented two elevations to the passer-by. Victorian window displays were highly imaginative, and a large window area was essential. On principal streets, such as Charing Cross Road, Victorian manufacturers established luxurious showrooms, where again large areas of glass allowed merchandise to be displayed. A good example of this is No. 148 Charing Cross Road, where James Hinks and Son, a manufacturer of brasswork and lighting, opted for large and decorative windows at first, second and third floor levels to maximise their display of lamps.

Hinks also ensured that the public spaces within their building were opulent. The elaborate vaulted ceiling and carved spiral staircase were details

Fig 46 Nos 18 and 19 Hanover Square in 1973, modern steel framed buildings

intended to suggest that their products were of a superior quality and design. Banking, another branch of commerce, used architectural detailing in a similar way. Once the modern system of branch banking had been established, much attention was paid to ensuring that the local branches of the major banks conveyed the same qualities of authority, pedigree and good judgement as their head offices did. The choice of Portland stone as a facing material to Nos 3 to 5 Oxford Street, for example, invited the customer to compare their bank to the great banking monuments of the City.

It is from such details that the history of buildings, and the needs and aspirations of their owners, may be teased. In the next chapter some of the buildings that helped produce the wealth on display in Victorian London are examined.

NOTES

1   Fig 30 based on Barker & Jackson 1990, 12-13; Bradley & Pevsner 1997, 44, 48, 413-626; Ekwall 1951, 81-7; Hurlen 1918, Porter 1994, 27 and Ross 2008a, 78, 81

2   Porter 1994, 136; Keily 2008, 90

3   Werner 2008a, 128-129

4   Thorpe, D. G. H. A history of English Clearing Banks, British Banking History Society, http://www.banking-history.co.uk/history.html [accessed: 02 April 2014]. The precursors to cheques were bills of exchange which had been used in Britain for inter-national trade from the 14th century onwards, but not used for domestic transfers until the 17th century. The first cheque used in Britain is thought to have been used in London in 1659; Cheque and Credit Clearing Company 2011, Cheques and cheque clearing: An historical perspective, 1-2 http://www.chequeandcredit.co.uk/files/candc/press/04_cheques_&_cheque_clearing_-_an_historical_perspective_v11_%28may11%29.pdf

5   Selds were covered market stalls that could either be attached to the front of buildings or freestanding structures with their own roofs.

6   This paragraph is largely drawn from Porter 1994, 199-202; Fig 31 is based on Harding and Keene 1987, 48-78 and People in Place 2003.

7   Williams (ed) 1933, 141-42

8   'Oxford Street: Introduction', in Survey of London: Volume 40, the Grosvenor Estate in Mayfair, Part 2 (The Buildings), ed. F H W Sheppard (London, 1980), p. 171 http://www.british-history.ac.uk/survey-london/vol40/pt2/p171 [accessed 11 August 2014].

9   Censuses of England and Wales 1841, and 1851; Registers of marriages St George, Bloomsbury (P82/GEO1/016-036)

10 Censuses of England and Wales 1841, and 1851; Parish Registers of St Leonard, Shoreditch.

11 Parish Registers of St James, Clerkenwell; Prerogative Court of Canterbury, will of Kyrle Ward.

12 Censuses of England and Wales 1851, and 1861; Parish Registers of St John, Richmond; Cemetery Register, All Souls Cemetery, Kensall Green.

13 Parish Registers of St George, Bloomsbury; *Calendar of Grants of Probate* 1882, William James Court, 'dealer in Gilders' materials'.

14 Censuses of England and Wales 1891, 1901 and 1911.

15 Richard Norman Shaw (b.1831-d.1912) was a British architect who designed country houses and commercial buildings from the 1870s to until 1908. His designs blended several styles including Neo-Baroque, Gothic Revival and an adaption of the 18th-century Queen Anne style. One of the buildings is most known for is his design of the New Scotland Yard building in London, which opened in 1890; Saint, A, 'Shaw, Richard Norman (1831–1912)', *Oxford Dictionary of National Biography*, Oxford University Press, 2004; online edn, Oct 2007 [http://www.oxforddnb.com/view/article/36050, accessed 25 Feb 2016]

16 Sherwell 1901, 6

CHAPTER 4

INDUSTRIAL LONDON

Introduction

London's well-developed medieval mercantile community (see Chapter 3) traded in the produce of the largest manufacturing centre in England. Many of its industries were those that would have been found in any medieval town: food and drink production, building, metalworking, clothing and textiles, tanning and leatherworking. The most important manufacturing district was Southwark, where cloth and leather industries were particularly strong. The 16th and 17th centuries saw the arrival of new industries brought by skilled immigrants, who could produce specialised goods such as Venetian-style glass, tin-glazed 'Delftware' pottery, and woven silk. During the first half of the 18th century London remained England's major manufacturing centre, enjoying the advantages of having the largest consumer market, the largest port, which facilitated the direct import of raw materials and export of manufactures, and a substantial pool of skilled labour that included many immigrant craftsmen.[1]

Ultimately, however, the high cost of land, coal and labour in the capital meant that the new industrial centres of the Midlands and the North could manufacture many goods more cheaply and London lost its predominance. Despite this, it continued to lead in the manufacture of specialised and luxury goods such as precision optical and scientific instruments, clocks and jewellery, porcelain, books, prints and engravings, and had a flourishing cabinet trade. Much of this work was still carried out in small factories and workshops by independent craftsmen. Particularly in the East End, however, the small industries also became associated with the practice of 'sweating', which made possible the mass-production of cheap consumer goods, such as clothing, footwear and furniture, by breaking production down into single processes that could be carried out by unskilled workers in their own homes, or in workshops set up in back rooms, garrets and cellars.[2]

More positively, London's pre-eminence as a port also created much employment in associated trades such as shipbuilding,[3] rope making and dock work. The sheer size of the London market meant that there was a constant demand for large quantities of food and drink, and brewing and milling were undertaken on a large scale close to the River Thames and the River Lea. The development of new technologies such as gas, electricity and railways, in the 19th century led to the creation of whole new industries and their associated infrastructure. London also developed a number of heavier industries, and noxious trades such as paint, oil, dye, soap and copperas works, which tended to congregate in the East End and on the south bank of the Thames.

Electricity

In the 19th century technology was developed to generate electricity and put it to practical uses. Over time it became a rival to gas lighting and by the 1920s had superseded it as a way of providing light for streets and homes. Electricity could also be used to power the telegraph and telephone technologies that emerged in the 19th century, and it revolutionised transport within the capital. In 1890 the first deep level underground railway with electric traction opened and by 1905 electric trams had replaced horse drawn trams. The earliest electrical goods for the home, including the refrigerator, electric heater, cooker and kettle, had been developed by 1912, although these were not generally taken up until after the Second World War.

The supply of electricity to London developed in a piecemeal fashion and was initially fraught with difficulties. The Electric Lighting Acts of 1882 and 1888 ensured that electricity companies stayed small in size and could only operate in a limited area. The Board of Trade also stipulated that local authorities in London would have a right to buy out any private electricity company in their district after 42 years. They were concerned that if one company could supply a city it would have too much influence over a local authority. At the same time the government recognised that it would probably be cheaper for electricity to be provided on a larger scale.

Stanford's map of London of 1890 shows the areas granted to the different electric light supply companies (Fig 47). It illustrates the confusing nature of early electricity supply, and the fact that in the late 19th century some districts (probably the more profitable ones) were supplied by several companies. Other areas, like the City of London and the East End, did not have any electrical supply at this time, relying instead on gas lighting provided by a number of coal gas works in East London. The driver for the eventual introduction of electricity to the East End during the 1890s was the campaign fought to improve the safety of the East End streets. West Ham Borough Council provided a general electrical supply for its area from 1898 and the Board of Works for Whitechapel began installing street lighting for that district from 1899.

By 1910 electricity was provided for London by a mixture of local authorities and private companies. The piecemeal provision of electricity was not co-ordinated until the establishment of connecting stations and the

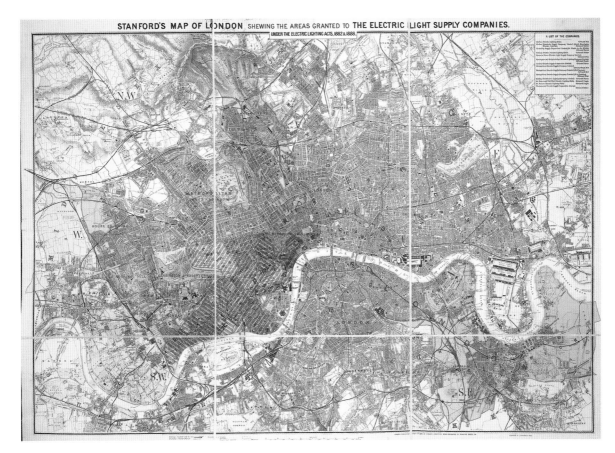

setting up of the National Grid in 1926. After this the supply of electricity was organised by the Central Electricity Board until nationalisation in 1948.

CROSSRAIL AND WHITE HART DEPOT ELECTRICITY GENERATING STATION

To deliver Crossrail services to Abbey Wood, a new tunnel has been built underneath the River Thames between North Woolwich and Plumstead. The tunnel stretches for almost two miles about 15m below the existing river bed and is the only point where the Crossrail route crosses the river. The portals at North Woolwich and Plumstead mark the entry and exit points for the tunnel.

At Plumstead a base was created for the engineering works associated with the Crossrail portal. This included an assembly point and access for the tunnel boring machines which were located on an area of land just north of the North Kent railway line. The Crossrail worksite lay within the southern part of the White Hart Depot, a Grade II Listed former electricity generating station, and the temporary removal of part of an original cobbled access ramp to the main depot building was required. The White Hart Depot (Gazetteer No. 147) is a substantial survival from an early 20th-century electricity

Fig 47 Stanford's map of London of 1890 showing the areas granted to London's electric light supply companies (British Library, Maps 3485/98)

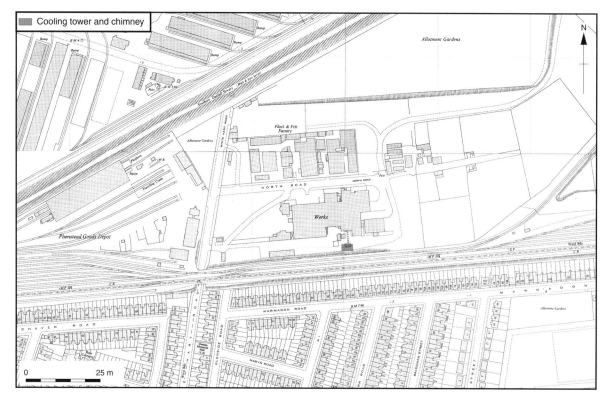

Cooling tower and chimney

Fig 48 The electricity generating station at White Hart Depot, Plumstead, on 1:1250 OS map of 1957/8, showing the layout of buildings and positions of the cooling tower and chimney (Groundsure)

generating station, which was fuelled by domestic rubbish and coal (Figs 48-50). Originally developed around 1898-9 by Plumstead Vestry, the plans were subsequently realised by the newly formed Metropolitan Borough of Woolwich. The plant was built between 1901 and 1903. Domestic rubbish and coal were burnt in furnaces that heated water boilers to create steam (Fig 51). The steam drove the turbines that generated the electricity. The scheme had the dual benefits for the local authority of providing cheaper electricity for street lighting, and a means of disposing of the borough's rubbish.

Fig 49 View of White Hart Depot main building looking from North Road

Fig 50 View of White Hart Depot main building looking south-east (Paul Talling)

Fig 51 Willesden Electricity Power Station, Engine House, 1900. Fuel (coal or domestic rubbish) was used to heat water in a nearby boiler house. Steam was taken from the boiler house and used to drive the turbines in the engine room, to generate electricity. A similar system would have operated at White Hart Road (Grace's Guide to British Industrial History)

The domestic rubbish was collected from the residents and businesses of the borough and brought to the plant by horse and cart for sorting by local women known as 'scratchers'. The coal was delivered by rail. Generation of electricity at White Hart Road ended in 1923 when the steam turbines and generators were removed (Fig 52). They were replaced by transformers, and White Hart Depot became a sub-station for the local distribution of electricity generated elsewhere. The furnaces and boilers continued in use to supply steam and hot water for a municipal laundry for local residents, and the borough's rubbish continued to be collected to fuel the furnaces or to be incinerated here until 1965. Subsequently the building has been used as a municipal depot and was Listed Grade II by Historic England in December 2000.

Groundworks for the construction of Crossrail's Plumstead Portal revealed parts of the bases of a chimney and a cooling tower of the former power

Fig 52 White Hart Depot; internal view of the tiled former generating hall within the main building

Fig 53 White Hart Depot: detail of the central area of the chimney structure, showing two solid brick bases to either side of a blackened area, which was an opening into the chimney for access

station (Fig 53), both part of the original layout of the generating plant and visible on the Ordnance Survey map of 1916 (see Fig 48). A large diameter cast iron pipe led from the base of the cooling tower and ran east past the chimney and turned slightly northward towards the wash mill and cooling tank to the east of the depot. The chimney was linked to the building to the north to take away the smoke from the furnaces powering the generators. On the south side of the chimney base there was access for clearing, cleaning and maintenance. Ashes and debris from the furnaces were removed via a narrow gauge railway.

Food Production

It is nine o'clock, and London has breakfasted…I want to know how many thousand eggs are daily chipped, how many of those embryo chickens are poached, and how many fried; how many tons of quartern loaves are cut up to make bread-and-butter, thick and thin; how many porkers have been sacrificed to provide the bacon rashers, fat and streaky; what rivers have been drained, what fuel consumed, what mounds of salt employed, what volumes of smoke emitted, to catch and cure the finny haddocks and the Yarmouth bloaters, that grace our morning repast.[4]

George Augustus Sala was wise to consider how much food was consumed in the capital and to wonder where it came from. London was and still is dependent on food produced in the British countryside, although in the 21st century 40% of the UK's food is imported from abroad.

The production of food in the countryside and supply to London allowed the Industrial Revolution to gain momentum in the capital. Over time fewer Londoners were involved in the food industry which allowed more of the population to be involved in manufacture or trade. In the 14th and 15th centuries 20% of Londoners were involved in processing food and drink, but by 1871 this had fallen to 2.74%.[5] This was made possible by the improvement in transport infrastructure, industrial-scale factory processing of food by machine, long life tinned foods and refrigeration.[6]

SMITHFIELD MARKET

Since medieval times London's main meat and livestock market had been located outside the city walls at Smithfield. Until the coming of the railways, livestock reared in the north and west of Britain, and fattened on the pasturelands of the Midlands and the Home Counties, had been driven to Smithfield on the hoof for slaughter and sale (Fig 54). Many of the animals were brought along the Great North Road, and towards

OLD SMITHFIELD.

Fig 54 Old Smithfield Market before closure in 1855 (Porter, c.1905, 130)

Smithfield along its final stretch, St John Street. By the early 19th century, however, there was a rising tide of protest, both at the filthy conditions, and the suffering of the animals:

Of all the horrid abominations with which London has been cursed, there is not one that can come up to that disgusting place, West Smithfield Market, for cruelty, filth, effluvia, pestilence, impiety, horrid language, danger, disgusting and shuddering sights, and every obnoxious item that can be imagined; and this abomination is suffered to continue year after year, from generation to generation, in the very heart of the most Christian and most polished city in the world.[7]

The railways were a much more efficient means of transporting both livestock and meat, and took a matter of hours rather than the days or weeks previously needed. With the opening of Kings Cross Station in 1850, the City authorities resolved to build a new livestock market at Copenhagen Fields in Islington to the north of the new station. The new market, known as the Metropolitan Cattle Market, was opened by Prince Albert in 1855, and for a decade the old market site at Smithfield was abandoned.

However, with the development of railways increasing quantities of meat were being brought to market as carcasses by rail. The meat market at Newgate to which this meat was directed was inconveniently sited and too limited in size, and the wagons carrying the meat from the railway stations blocked the nearby streets.

In 1860 the City authorities decided to construct a new Metropolitan Meat Market at Smithfield. This was developed on a cleared site immediately to the north of the old market, and to the south-west of Charterhouse Square. The market was developed in conjunction with the extension of the Metropolitan Railway, the world's first underground line, which was constructed from Paddington to Farringdon between 1860 and 1863 and extended through Aldersgate (now Barbican) to Moorgate in the City by 1865. It was designed to link Paddington, Euston and Kings Cross stations with the City, and relieve congestion on the roads by providing an underground rail link for commuters and goods. Extensive sidings were built allowing carcasses to be transferred directly by rail from the mainline stations to Smithfield Market or to cold storage.

The new market, initially consisting of the Central East and West Markets, was opened in 1868. Between 1873 and 1876 a new Poultry Market was built to the west (subsequently burnt down and replaced in the 1960s), and the site of the old livestock market was laid out with a rotunda, gardens and a fountain. The General Market was added between 1879 and 1883 for fruit and vegetables, to replace the old Farringdon Market; the Fish Market was added in 1888, followed by the Red House, built in 1898-9 for the London Central Markets Cold Storage Co. Ltd., one of the first cold stores to be built outside the London docks (Figs 55–56).[8]

Fig 55 Smithfield Market in 2014 showing the Central East and West Markets, Poultry Market, General Market, Fish Market and Red House with railway lines

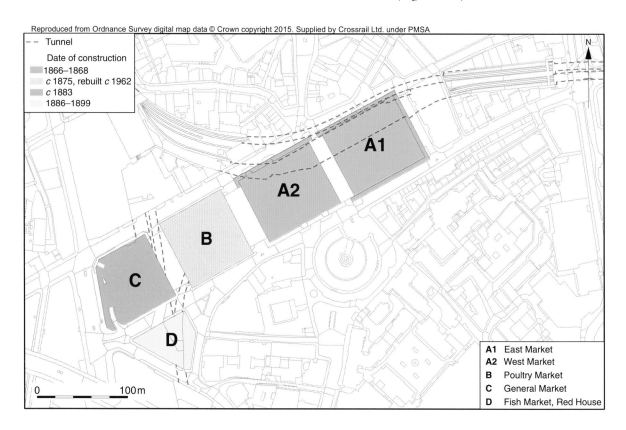

- – Tunnel

Date of construction
- 1866–1868
- c 1875, rebuilt c 1962
- c 1883
- 1886–1899

N

A1

A2

B

C

D

0   100m

A1	East Market
A2	West Market
B	Poultry Market
C	General Market
D	Fish Market, Red House

THE CHANGING FACE OF LONDON

METROPOLITAN MEAT MARKET.

Fig 56 Smithfield Market in the late 19th century. Porter, *c*.1905, 130

CROSSRAIL AND SMITHFIELD

Farringdon Station is undergoing extensive rebuilding as part of the Crossrail and Thameslink projects, and will be the only station where the two lines intersect. The construction of a new ticket hall (the Eastern Ticket Hall) in the area immediately to the east of Smithfield Market required the demolition of a number of late 19th- and 20th-century buildings, which were recorded prior to removal (Fig 57). The works associated with the construction of the Metropolitan railway lines in the 1860s had led to wholesale reorganisation of this area, including the creation of two new side streets, Lindsey Street and Hayne Street, to the north of the older Long Lane. Inevitably, the area had become a focus of meat processing and wholesale distribution, and the buildings recorded for Crossrail were closely, although not exclusively, associated with this trade.

This block of commercial and industrial buildings also benefited from being directly above two train stations, Aldersgate (now Barbican) and the goods yard and station at Smithfield Market. The goods yard under Smithfield market remained until 1962 (Fig 58).

NOS 20-23 LONG LANE AND NO. 2 LINDSEY STREET

At the east end of Smithfield Market this block of three large four-storey structures (Gazetteer No. 112) was first constructed in the late 19th

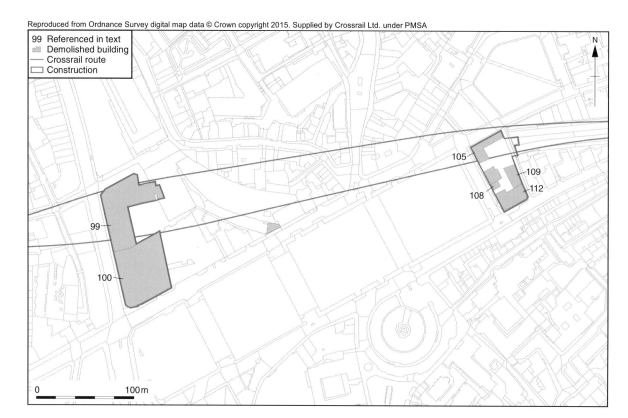

Fig 57 Map showing the location of buildings demolished for the construction of the new Crossrail Farringdon Station east and west ticket halls. Buildings discussed in the text are shown in blue and labelled with their gazetteer numbers

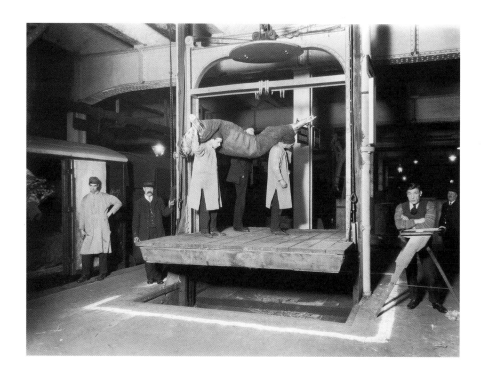

Fig 58 Smithfield Goods Depot in 1926; the lift is being used to move meat from the railway platform up to Smithfield Market (National Railway Museum/Science & Society Picture Library)

Fig 59 (left) No. 22 Long Lane; (right) No. 20 Long Lane

century. Historic trade directories show that the structures originally housed a number of businesses, with No. 21 Long Lane being in use as a butchers, No. 22 as a gold blockers, and No. 23 was a Temperance hotel.

A photograph of the building prior to conversion in the 1940s published in The Builder in 1945 suggests that, at the time of survey for Crossrail, No. 20 Long Lane preserved some evidence of the original appearance of the block. It was four storeys high with red brick and painted stone dressings, although it had been completely modernised on the ground floor. The canted corner contained windows on each floor, which must have been inserted at a later date (Fig 59).

NO. 3 LINDSEY STREET

To the north was No. 3 Lindsey Street (Gazetteer No. 108), a single-storey late 19th-century structure with a timber louvre and a series of shallow hipped roofs (Fig 60).

This building, and its complex relationship with other structures in the area, is illustrated by a plan drawn up in 1918 in advance of the extension of the Great Western Railway's facilities here (Fig 61). At this time No. 3 Lindsey Street was in use as a condemned meat store. Around the outside of the building was a public lavatory with an attendant's room. To the south, No. 2 Lindsey Street was labelled London Central Hotel with a yard behind.

Fig 60 No. 3 Lindsey Street in 2009

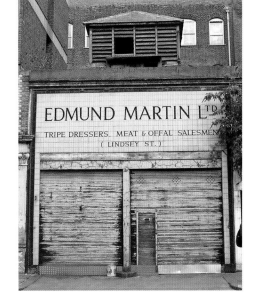

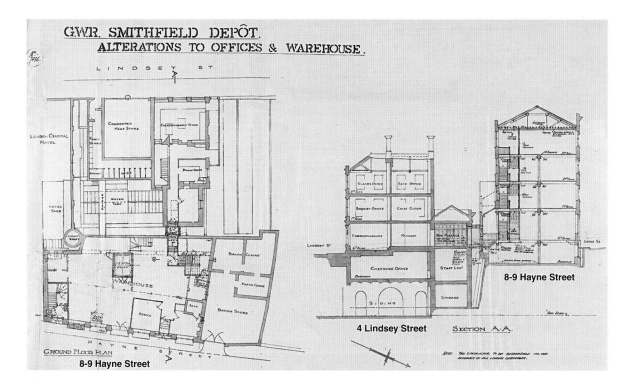

GWR. SMITHFIELD DEPÔT.
ALTERATIONS TO OFFICES & WAREHOUSE.

LINDSEY ST.

8-9 Hayne Street

4 Lindsey Street   SECTION A·A·

GROUND FLOOR PLAN
8-9 Hayne Street

Fig 61 A plan of proposed alterations to the Great Western Railway depot at Smithfield in 1918. No. 3 Lindsey Street is labelled as a condemned meat store (London Metropolitan Archives, GLC/AR/BR/22/BA/043620)

The Great Western Railway saw a great opportunity in having a direct connection to the new Smithfield Market, and ensured that an extensive GWR depot was established on the site. Using the Metropolitan Line by agreement, it was soon transporting meat and other goods from its core territories to the new London market. No. 4 Lindsey Street was the company's office, although it was later to expand into other buildings in the block. Access to the sidings and platform area was beneath No. 3. A surviving stone pilaster on the left-hand side of the facade of No. 3 that can be seen on Figure 60 was all that remained of the Great Western Railway office at the time of Crossrail's record of the building.

NOS 8-9 HAYNE STREET

Nos 8-9 Hayne Street (Gazetteer No. 109) comprised a late Victorian warehouse building, seven bays wide and four storeys high, with the later addition of a modern attic storey concealed by a parapet (Fig 62).

In 1910 the building was used by a printer and bookbinder. A bacon store is shown to the north in 1918, when the Great Western Railway absorbed Nos 8-9 into its operations, and constructed a ground floor bridge linking it to the back of No. 4 Lindsey Street. A lift was also inserted to link the warehouse with the platform level beneath, enabling goods to be moved directly from the railway. At the same time, the company acquired a similar warehouse on the opposite side of the road

Fig 62 Nos 8-9 Hayne Street: left) the street frontage, right) detail of the rear of the building showing blocked doorway and the remains of the bridge constructed by the Great Western Railway to link to the back of No. 4 Lindsey Street

at No. 2 Hayne Street, and constructed another bridge to link the two buildings. This bridge was removed in 1932.

ARMOUR AND CO.

By 1938 the Chicago-based American meat importers Armour and Co. Ltd appear to have taken over several buildings in the area, including the block in Long Lane and Lindsey Street, part of which was subsequently remodelled in Art Deco style (Figs 63-64).

One of the company's specialisms was canning meat and it is likely to have been one of the official meat suppliers during the Second World War. The company expanded in the 1950s into Nos 8-9 Hayne Street and the two properties were linked with a bridge. Armour and Co. developed a system that started with the collection of meat from the railway station below ground, from where it was transported via a lift into Nos 8-9 Hayne Street for processing. The processed meat was then taken across the bridge and down via a lift into the wholesale shop on Long Lane and Lindsey Street.

Fig 63 Nos 22-23 Long Lane in use by Armour and Co., Chicago-based meat importers, prior to the building's conversion in the 1940s (English Heritage, Archives, BL 28770)

54-64 CHARTERHOUSE STREET (SMITHFIELD HOUSE)

This L-shaped building, called Smithfield House (Gazetteer No. 105), was constructed in 1930 in period style and was built as offices and workshops (Figs. 65-66). A loading bay was included. On the eastern elevation the building had loading doors which would have allowed goods to be unloaded from a rear yard.

Fig 64 The corner of the block at (left) No. 2 Lindsey Street and (right) No. 23 Long Lane remodelled in Art Deco style, as it survived prior to demolition in 2009

There was evidence for a travelling crane operating between Smithfield House and the warehouse at No. 10 Hayne Street. This could have been employed by Armour & Co Ltd who used the building as a goods yard for their nearby meat processing workshops and warehouses during the mid 20th century.

One of the most interesting aspects of this building was uncovered during its demolition, when it was revealed that it had been constructed on a steel lattice which suspended the building above the railway line below (Fig 67). The construction of this steel lattice in the early 20th century is instructive as it shows that this area was commercially profitable enough to invest in such heavy-duty infrastructure.

Fig 65 Nos 54-64 Charterhouse Street (Smithfield House)

Fig 66 Nos 54-64 Charterhouse Street (Smithfield House) rear view

East End London industries

The building up of the East End of London gathered pace during the period of rapid population expansion in the late 16th century. Over the next hundred years, the East End grew faster than any other area of London, and by 1680 it is estimated that there were 140,000 people living here. Ships and boats had been built and repaired along the Thames east of the City since the medieval period, but shipbuilding and related industries in the area developed rapidly following Henry VIII's creation of naval dockyards in the 16th century, the establishment of the East India Company's docks at Blackwall in 1614, and the progressive expansion of England's maritime trade. Housing for the workers in shipbuilding, docking and associated trades spread along the Thames through St Katherine's, Wapping, Shadwell and Limehouse, nearly as far as Blackwall itself. One of the trades most closely associated with the early East End was silk weaving, which expanded enormously following the arrival in the area of thousands of French Huguenots fleeing religious persecution. By 1687 over 13,000 had come to London and many were highly skilled silk weavers. Most settled in Spitalfields, but as their community grew some moved outwards to Bethnal Green and Mile End Town. They benefited from being located close to the Thames, where they could receive a steady

Fig 67 The demolition of Nos 54-64 Charterhouse Street (Smithfield House) revealed the steel decking structure that had suspended the building over the railway lines below

supply of raw material. Silk weaving became one of the main industries in Spitalfields but the reliance of the community on this one trade brought poverty during the early 19th century as Spitalfields weavers were unable to compete with the mills of Lancashire and Cheshire.

By the 18th century the City was ringed on the east by a dense band of new suburbs, stretching from Shoreditch in the north-east, southwards through Spitalfields and Whitechapel to East Smithfield and the riverside areas of Ratcliff and Shadwell. The Thames-side parishes of Wapping, Shadwell, Limehouse and Ratcliff had become centres of maritime commerce and industry on a large scale (Fig 68). The industries that developed around the docks included timber yards, coal yards,

Fig 68 Thames-side industries in the East End, from John Rocque's Map of London, Westminster and Southwark of 1746 (MOTCO)

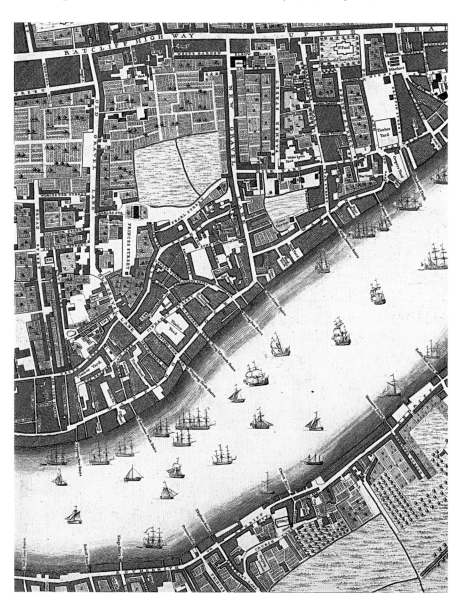

THE CHANGING FACE OF LONDON

shipbuilding, rope making and sugar refining, along with very substantial growth in brewing and distilling throughout the East End.

Just as significantly for the future, however, the East End had long been a place where some of the more unpleasant trades were located. Not only were the offensive sights and smells of these trades removed downwind from the City and the West End, but there was cheap land and labour available for expansion. Here, large numbers of slaughterhouses provided animal carcasses for processing for tallow and glue, and hides for tanning. Other trades that were established in the East End included the making of dyes, ink, paint and tar.[9]

Another industry that was initially confined to the outskirts of the city was brewing. By the 15th century breweries had set up to the east of the Tower of London, outside the city walls and adjacent to the Thames for a guaranteed water supply. By the 18th century London had some of the largest breweries in the country and by the 19th century brewing was one of London's primary manufacturing industries and was dominated by around twelve companies.[10] One of the largest and longest running breweries was the Black Eagle Brewery at Spitalfields run by Truman, Hanbury, Buxton & Co Ltd. This brewery was founded in 1669 and some of its buildings still survive and have been converted into an independent shopping complex at 91 Brick Lane.

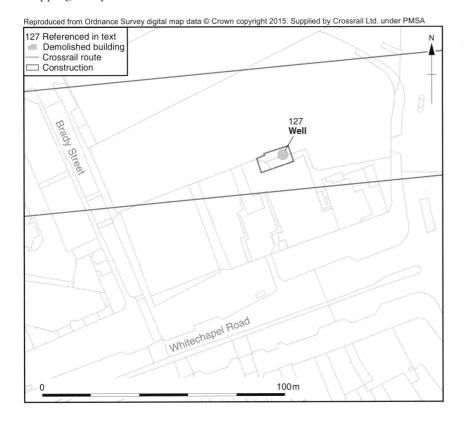

Reproduced from Ordnance Survey digital map data © Crown copyright 2015. Supplied by Crossrail Ltd. under PMSA

127 Referenced in text
Demolished building
Crossrail route
Construction

127
Well

N

Brady Street

Whitechapel Road

0   100m

Fig 69 Plan showing the location of Crossrail works at the Albion Brewery, Whitechapel

The route of Crossrail beneath the East End passes the sites of many of these industries, for instance the Black Eagle Brewery is located 155m north of Crossrail. Only rarely would industrial activity have had an effect on deposits deep below the surface, but brewing, an industry requiring deep wells to provide clean water, was one example. The Albion Brewery's artesian well (Gazetteer No. 127), which is almost 200 metres deep and lined with riveted cast iron panelling, was recorded by Crossrail in advance of the start of construction.[11] The well was located in the basement of the Grade II Listed Albion Brewery building in Whitechapel (Figs 69–70).

The Albion Brewery was built in 1808 by Richard Ivory, the landlord of the nearby Blind Beggar public house. The brewery changed ownership a number of times but in the mid 19th century was mainly owned by the Mann and Crossman families. In 1860 the brewery was producing 133,000 barrels of beer each year and 700,000 by 1919. In 1958 the company merged with Watney, Combe, Reid and Co Ltd, London to form Watney Mann Ltd. The Albion Brewery operated until its closure in 1979.

Fig 70 Lined shaft of the artesian well revealed during excavations for Crossrail at the Albion Brewery, Whitechapel

Beyond the River Lea

The countryside east of the River Lea remained largely rural until the 19th century. It no doubt continued to resemble the landscape Rocque depicted in 1746; with a patchwork of irregular enclosed fields, market gardens and the villages of Stratford, West Ham, Plaistow and Poplar (Fig. 71).

The transformation of this rural area into a heavily urbanised and polluted industrial townscape by the end of the 19th century was as fast as it was dramatic. In 1740, with around 570 householders, the population of the largest village, West Ham, may have been around 2000-2500; by 1801 it had increased to 6,485, doubling to 12,738 by 1841, to reach a pheno-menal 289,000 by 1911. Most of the growth took place between 1871 and 1901, when the population of West Ham alone increased by over 200,000.[12]

The growth of the area was promoted by a number of different factors. The railway arrived in the region in 1839, and it soon became a major junction, with the workshops of the Eastern Counties Railway and the North London Railway established in Stratford and Bow. respectively. The railways created thousands of new jobs in the area.

Despite the impact of the railways, however, the single most important stimulus to the development of the area was the continuing expansion

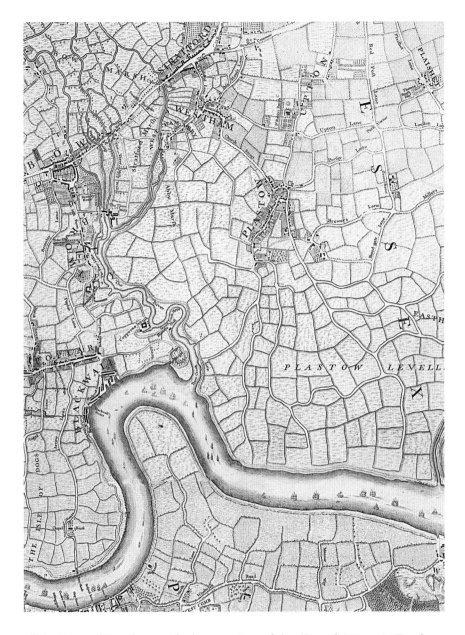

Fig 71 Jean Rocque's map of the countryside east of the River Lea in 1746 (British Library, Maps. Crace XIX/18)

of the Port of London, with the opening of the (Royal) Victoria Dock in the Thames marshes between West Ham and North Woolwich in 1855, followed by the Royal Albert Dock by 1880.[13] These two docks alone provided work for around 3000 people by the end of the 19th century, but they also acted as a stimulus to other trades. Most importantly, coal brought to the docks by sea was 40% cheaper than coal brought by rail, allowing East End factories to compete with the factories of the Midlands and the North.[14]

The railways, the docks, the River Lea and the availability of cheap and agriculturally unproductive marshland provided the ideal conditions for industry, with plenty of space for new and expanded works to be serviced by the rapidly developing transport infrastructure. In the 1860s, 'the landowners in Plaistow Marsh and the adjoining marsh-land were jointly seeking professional advice on how their property might be drained sufficiently to permit building on it, since they thought it suitable for working-class dwellings and the establishment of obnoxious trades which it was desired to expel from London'.[15]

Fig 72 Stanford's map of 1862 shows the building-up and industrialisation of East London, as new manufacturing and service works were set up, along with new terraces of housing for the growing working population. (MOTCO)

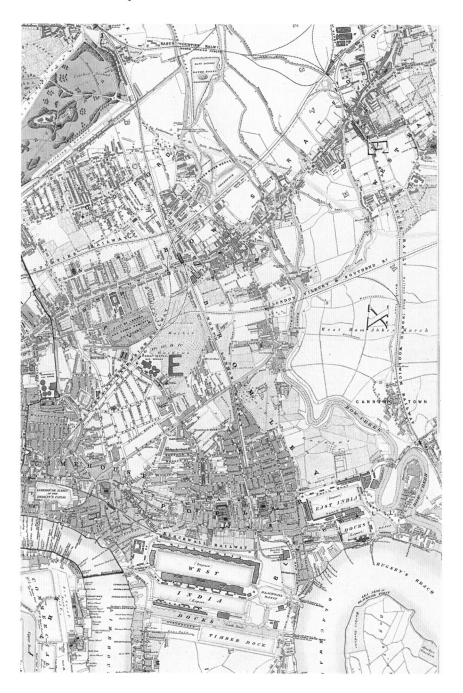

The steady build-up of industry alongside surviving areas of market gardens in the 1860s and 1870s can be seen on Stanford's maps of 1862 and 1872 along with the new terraces of housing being built for the growing industrial population (Fig 72).

The maps illustrate the range of manufacturing and service works becoming established in the area, notably the carriage sheds of the North London Railway, the West Ham and Great Central Gas Works, tanning and leather works, several chemical works, starch works, a manure works, tar works, rubber works, iron foundries, lime kilns, printers, mills and distilleries. In 1910 West Ham Borough Council was calling itself 'the factory centre of the south of England'.[16] The chemical industries remained the single largest group, producing coke, tar and turpentine, creosote, disinfectants, perfumes and cosmetics, sulphuric acid, paint, varnish, dye, printing ink and matches. The processing of animal and vegetable oils for tallow, soap, glues and fertilisers involved some of the most offensive operations. Engineering and metalworking remained important, with the railways and shipbuilding providing important local markets. By the second half of the 19th century the area's earlier calico printing industry was giving way to the manufacture of coarser textiles and jute spinning, and West Ham was an early centre of rubber production. Printing, food processing and timber milling were also growing. The largest factories tended to be located along the Thames, in the district of Silvertown. These included chemical works, rubber works, iron works and the sugar refineries of Henry Tate & Sons from 1877, and of Abram Lyle & Sons from 1881.[17]

At Stratford and near Stratford Bridge, in an awfully evil-smelling place called Marsh Gate Lane, there are several lucifer-match manufactories, at which the hands employed appear to be chiefly females… I spoke to one girl, about sixteen years old, and she told me that she lived in Shadwell (about two miles distant), and that working twelve hours a day she could earn seven shillings a week, out of which she gave her mother half a crown a week for her lodging and washing, and "kep' herself in food and clothes with the remaining four-and-sixpence.[18]

EAST LONDON SOAP WORKS

The area around Pudding Mill Lane was one of the areas used by heavy industries by the end of the 19th century. Three of the buildings surveyed by Crossrail in advance of constructon commencing were previously part of the East London Soap Works (Gazetteer No. 133) (Fig 73). This establishment was owned by Edward Cook & Company, manufacturers of soap, tallow and fertilisers, and they were operating on Cooks Road in Bow by 1862 (Figs 74–75). In that year they had a stand at the International Exhibition and were producing 'Yellow, mottled, curd and soft soaps'.

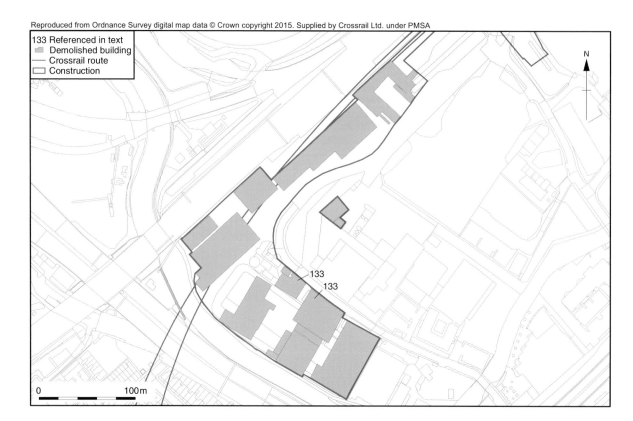

133 Referenced in text
▨ Demolished building
— Crossrail route
▢ Construction

N

0   100m

Fig 73 Plan showing the former East London Soap Works, Cooks Road, Bow

The East London Soap Works benefited from its location close to the railways and the River Lea. The expansion of the works can be followed on the Ordnance Survey maps of the late 19th century, first appearing in 1862. The 1867 map suggests that the works had already expanded over part of the former gas works alongside the GER embankment, accessed by Five Bells Bridge and by the road later known as Cooks Road. On the north side of the works was a large house set in formal gardens, with a small rectangular building on the north side of the main gate. It is possible that these may have been Marlborough House and the Gate House, known to

Fig 74 An advertisement for the East London Soap Works at Bow, 1862 (Grace's Guide to British Industrial History)

Fig 75 An advertisement from 1904 for Lasso Soap, made at the East London Soap Works at Bow (Grace's Guide to British Industrial History)

THE CHANGING FACE OF LONDON

have stood in this area, and possibly the owner's house with a coach house and stabling. By 1916 the works had grown to perhaps its maximum extent. The earlier production building had been replaced by a much larger soap factory, and a group of new buildings had appeared. Three of these survived at the time of the Crossrail investigations and were surveyed before demolition. The first building was used as a house, probably for a member of staff (Fig 76) and this abutted one to the south which was used for several purposes in its history including a factory, stores and offices.

The third building was a separate factory building. Evidence suggested that this had housed an overhead travelling crane for loading goods into rail trucks (Fig 77). In 1916 this building had a rail link with the larger East London Soap Factory building to the north-west. This connected the factory buildings to the main line railway where Pudding Mill Station is now located.

The commercial growth of London during the 17th and 18th centuries was interwoven with the development of its industries, particularly those of shipbuilding and the production of clothing and luxury goods. Although the later 18th-century emergence of industrial powerhouses in the Midlands and the North put paid to London's industrial dominance it continued to be a city of great industry. The rapid growth in London's population after 1800 created a huge demand for its goods and services,

Fig 76 The former East London Soap Works, Bow; probable staff house and attached office building

Fig 77 The former East London Soap Works, Bow; interior of a factory building with evidence of travelling crane rails

both internally and externally. The task of provisioning this rising population fell to the railways, which from the 1830s had emerged as the fastest way to connect the city with its hinterland. The Great Western Railway took full advantage of its interests in the Metropolitan Railway, ensuring that as the new Smithfield Meat Market emerged during the 1860s it was their railway which controlled the extensive goods facilities beneath the market. Crossrail's construction of a station at Farringdon has shed light on some of the ancillary services that naturally developed to service Smithfield's meat trade. The industrial scale of meat processing and wholesale distribution that building recording work to the east of Smithfield has revealed was a direct result of the ease with which meat could be unloaded from the GWR's wagons and transferred into neighbouring factories.

Rail connections such as this quickly became an essential requirement for any London company with large or bulky cargoes to transport. Like Armour & Co's premises at Smithfield, the East London Soap Works in Bow had internal rail access, with its own lifting equipment to load and unload goods, as did White Hart Depot, the electricity generating station at Plumstead. White Hart Depot was an example of the new industrial premises that began to emerge as the Victorian period drew to a close. The production of electricity quickly became an industry in its own right, and many jobs were created in the fields of distribution and maintenance. Local electricity sub-stations helped the widespread take-up of the new power during the first years of the 20th century, and ensured that as officework gradually started to replace manual labour, offices, the new workplaces of London, had ready supplies of the new power. In the next chapter the rise of the purpose-built office in London is examined.

NOTES

1   Schofield 2008, 80-81; Lister, 2008, 132-3.

2   Porter 1994, 140-41; Hoffbrand, 2008, 214.

3   Harrison 2015

4   Sala 1862, 78.

5   The industrialisation of food production, particularly the growth and development of Crosse & Blackwell, one of London's foremost former food producers, is a subject covered in Jeffries *et al.*, forthcoming.

6   Census of England and Wales, 1871, *Population abstracts. Ages, civil condition, occupations, and birth-places of the people. Vol. III* BPP 1873 LXXI Pt. I. Population abstracts, England and Wales, Vol. III, 1871] Division 1. London: Including parts of Middlesex, Surrey and Kent 3, 12 URL: http://www.histpop.org (date accessed 30 September 2015)

7   Maslen 1843, 16

8   Fig 55 after Barton 2008, 3-4 and City of London 2014, History of Smithfield Market

9   Werner 2008b, 170-171

10 Marriott 2011, 22, 28, 35-8, 55-6; Porter 1994, 195-96

11 An artesian well is a well that is dug into a confined aquifer. The pressure in the aquifer pushes the water up the well without the need for pumping.

12 'West Ham: Introduction', in A History of the County of Essex: Volume 6, ed. W R Powell (London, 1973), pp. 43-50 http://www.british-history.ac.uk/vch/essex/vol 6/ pp43-50 [accessed 9 September 2015].

13 'West Ham: Rivers, bridges, wharfs and docks', in *A History of the County of Essex: Volume 6*, ed. W R Powell (London, 1973), pp. 57-61 http://www.british-history.ac.uk/vch/essex/vol6/pp57-61 [accessed 10 September 2015].

14 'Economic influences on growth: Employment opportunities', in *A History of the County of Essex: Volume 5*, ed. W R Powell (London, 1966), pp. 9-21 http://www.british-history.ac.uk/vch/essex/vol5/pp9-21 [accessed 10 September 2015].

15 loc. cit.

16 *West Ham, the factory centre of the south of England. c.1910.*

17 'West Ham: Industries', in *A History of the County of Essex:* Volume 6, ed. W R Powell (London, 1973), pp. 76-89 http://www.british-history.ac.uk/vch/essex/vol6/pp76-89 [accessed 9 September 2015].

18 'By One of the crowd' [James Greenwood] 1883, 8-9.

CHAPTER 5

THE RISE OF THE PURPOSE-BUILT OFFICE

The office is perhaps most easily defined as a room, or suite of rooms, used for non-manual work. Today, both at home and in the workplace, the tasks of document and spreadsheet generation, administration and management, co-ordinated from a computer work-station, are commonplace. For modern companies, computer-generated digital files are the tool for internal organisation and communication, and the currency through which transactions with the world are realised and recorded.

Crossrail's state of the art offices are on the 28th to 30th floors of 25 Canada Square, Canary Wharf (Fig 78). This is the hub of a project employing over 10,000 people spread over 40 sites within one of the busiest cities in the world.[1] By January 2014 the progress and co-ordination of Crossrail had generated over 430,000 administrative documents.

Externally No. 25 Canada Square is impressive, for the building stands 200m high and has 45 storeys above a marble-floored lobby. However, internally Crossrail's offices are typical of those of many large modern corporations. The working areas are largely open plan and utilitarian and comprise little more complex than rows of computer work-stations, with partitions and sub-divisions to provide for reception areas, meeting rooms, etc. The only other spaces required are toilets and refreshment facilities. There is little to distinguish the function of any particular department or the relative seniority of any staff. Indeed each of the three floors, and each wing of each floor, appears confusingly alike to the casual observer.

Fig 78 25 Canada Square, Canary Wharf. Crossrail's offices are located on the 28th to 30th floors. (Citigroup/Sectorlight Marketing & Design Ltd)

Some of the characteristics of the Crossrail management centre have long been integral to the administrative workplace; others are a more recent product of evolving technologies and changing attitudes to working relationships. The recording of buildings affected by the construction of Crossrail included some interesting structures that help illustrate the changing world of the office.

The origins of the office

Gideon Haigh, in his global review *The Office: A Hardworking History*[2] begins with a depiction of an administrative room on a relief from Ancient Egypt and moves forward through the writing rooms of monasteries and the merchant counting halls of the medieval period and continues with the Palazzo Uffizi, the name of which translates literally as office building, and which was built for the Florentine magistrates at the instigation of Cosimo I de' Medici.

Closer to home, the Old Admiralty Building (now Ripley House, 1726) in Whitehall, is one of the earliest purpose built offices in London. Other early examples are the government offices at Somerset House (1775-1780) and the East India Company's East India House, in Leadenhall Street (completed in 1729 and demolished in 1861). These can be viewed as the precursors of large modern purpose-built corporate offices. East India House was the administrative centre for the East India Company, which was not only a huge international commercial operation, but also governed large parts of India and maintained its own military and naval forces. As well as providing the necessary office accommodation, the solidity of the Georgian facade of East India House expressed to the world and perhaps more importantly to shareholders and potential investors, a sense of its gravitas and permanence.

Early industrial enterprises were run by their owners assisted by overseers and had little need for extensive office space, but as businesses grew and expanded the need for records of transactions inevitably grew and with it the need for more clerical and administrative 'white collar' workers. The numbers of these workers increased enormously in the 19th century. The figures recorded in the census returns just for business and commercial clerks and excluding other white-collar workers are instructive. In 1841 the number of commercial or business clerks in England and Wales was 56,830 of which number only 152 were women, by 1891 the number of clerks was 247,229, including 17,859 women. In 1911 the number of commercial and business clerks was 477,535 including 117,057 women.[3]

East India House may have been an imposing building but the work of clerks within its walls was little different from that of any other office. Charles Lamb (1775-1834) the essayist and friend of Coleridge, Wordsworth, Hazlitt and others, worked as a clerk in the Accountant's Department of the East India Company for 33 years until his retirement in 1825. In a letter to Wordsworth in 1822 he wrote:

I grow ominously tired of official confinement. Thirty years have I served the Philistines, and my neck is not subdued to the yoke. You don't know how wearisome it is to breathe the air of four pent walls without relief day after day all the golden hours of the day between 10 and 4 without ease or interposition.[4]

Charles Dickens is the best known of the authors who have described the working life of the urban population. He had first-hand experience of offices, as his working life included a period as a clerk to a firm of solicitors in Gray's Inn. Later he worked as a reporter and sketch writer for several newspapers. He frequently used the office or counting house as a backdrop in works such as *Nicholas Nickleby* and *Our Mutual Friend*, but most famously in *A Christmas Carol*, which provides a graphic image of the bleak environment and depressing drudgery that could be the lot of the clerk (Fig 79). In Sketches from Boz, Dickens describes his idea of a typical office clerk:

Fig 79 Bob Cratchit working by candle light at the offices of Scrooge and Marley (Victorian Web www.victorianweb.org)

We thought we almost saw the dingy little back office into which he walks every morning, hanging his hat on the same peg, and placing his legs beneath the same desk: first, taking off that black coat which lasts the year through, and putting on the one which did duty last year, and which he keeps in his desk to save the other. There he sits till five o'clock, working on, all day, as regularly as the dial over the mantel-piece, whose loud ticking is as monotonous as his whole existence: only raising his head when some one enters the counting-house, or when, in the midst of some difficult calculation, he looks up to the ceiling as if there were inspiration in the dusty skylight with a green knot in the centre of every pane of glass. About five, or half-past, he slowly dismounts from his accustomed stool, and again changing his coat, proceeds to his usual dining-place, somewhere near Bucklersbury.[5]

The second half of the 19th century was a time of dramatic change. London was the centre of an empire and the world's largest city. Between 1831 and 1901 Greater London's population grew from 1,729,949 to 6,226,494.[6] This was an age of reform, and the response to the overcrowding, poor sanitation and generally poor living conditions caused by rapid population growth was the re-organisation of local government followed by legislation addressing and improving sanitation and drainage, and living and working conditions.[7]

Crossrail and the office building

NOS 11-12 BLOMFIELD STREET

Property entrepreneurs, particularly in the City and West End, realised that there were opportunities to create bespoke office accommodation to let. An early example at Nos 11-12 Blomfield Street recorded by Crossrail was a long way from Bob Cratchit's cold and dimly illuminated work space.

This office building was located near to Liverpool Street in the City (Gazetteer No. 117) (Fig 80). It opened in 1887, the year of Queen Victoria's

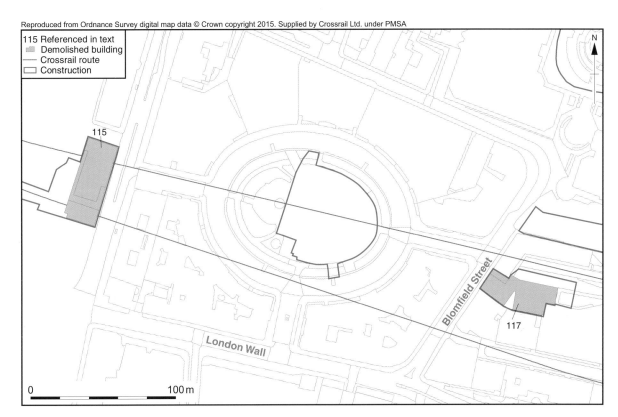

115 Referenced in text
▨ Demolished building
— Crossrail route
▢ Construction

115

Blomfield Street

117

London Wall

0   100 m

N

Fig. 80 Plan showing the location of Nos 11-12 Blomfield Street. Buildings discussed in the text are shown in blue and labelled with their gazetteer numbers (Oxford Archaeology/Ramboll)

Golden Jubilee. It comprised two linked structures aligned east–west: The first, Nos 11–12 Blomfield Street, comprised open plan office space on five floors, with a lower ground floor and attic space (Fig 81). This structure had been built using iron column frame construction, a system made fashionable by Joseph Paxton with construction of the Crystal Palace for the Great Exhibition of 1851. There were light wells to provide natural light. Elaborate fixtures and fittings adorned the entrance, hall, doorways and stairs. The upper floors were accessed by a geometric staircase decorated with colourful ceramic tiles (Fig 82) and extensive use was made of decorated stone and dark hardwoods like mahogany as well as ceramic tiles (Fig 83). The second structure, which fronted onto Broad Street Avenue to the west, was a building with five floors, and an attic, a lower ground floor and a basement. The upper floors were accessed by means of a cantilevered stairway. Corridors on each floor ran east–west with offices to the north and south. The corridors linked to those in the 11–12 Blomfield Street building. Again there were light wells to provide natural light.

A surprise find made by the archaeologists recording the Blomfield Street building was a hydraulic lift, the remains of which were found at the base

Fig. 81 Nos 11-12 Blomfield Street in 2004 prior to demolition

THE RISE OF THE PURPOSE-BUILT OFFICE

Fig 82 (left) Nos 11-12 Blomfield Street: geometric staircase

Fig 83 (right) Nos 11-12 Blomfield Street: elaborate internal entrances

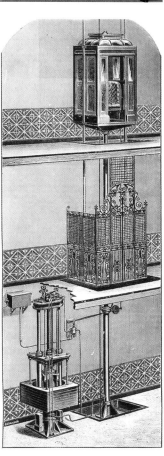

Fig 84a (left) Nos 11-12 Blomfield Street: The hand crank for hydraulic lift found below the geometric staircase

Fig 84a (right) A direct acting hydraulic lift (Grace's Guide to British Industrial History)

of the geometric staircase. This lift would have been the most up-to-date technology in the 1880s. The lift may have been supplied by Richard Waygood & Co Ltd, one of the largest suppliers of hydraulic direct action passenger lifts in Britain in the 1880s (Fig 84). Waygood & Co made use of high pressure water supply by the London Hydraulic Power Company. Pressure was stored up in an accumulator and released when the lift was needed. Waygood & Co introduced their Automatic Water-Saving Lift and Hoist in 1894 with a governor valve which regulated the amount of water usage according to the weight of the load.[8]

Lifts were a good investment for owners leasing out purpose-built office blocks in the late 19th century. Commercial buildings without lifts would have variable rents for different floors, with the ground floor being the most expensive and the top floor the cheapest. The invention of reliable passenger lifts by the 1880s meant that the rental income for upper floors could be increased, therefore increasing the profits of the whole building.

The building was owned by the Salaman family which had made its fortune from the international trade in ostrich feathers. In 1895 the building housed 40 businesses in 73 offices. The businesses included a range of multi-national enterprises such as the Mexican Southern Railway Ltd, Elmore's German & Austro-Hungarian Metal Co. Ltd, and the Coruna, Santiago & Peninsular Railway Co. Ltd as well as the office of the Consul-General for the Orange Free State. The buildings seem to have provided small but well-appointed office spaces particularly for foreign and international businesses requiring office space in London.

Fig 85 The entrance to Nos 9-15 Oxford Street

NOS 9-15 OXFORD STREET

The range at Nos 9-15 Oxford Street (Gazetteer No. 83; Fig 32) comprised a single block of four bays with a basement, ground floor and three upper floors including an attic floor under a mansard roof. The east bay tower, which had a fourth floor, provided stair access to the upper floors. As with Nos 11-12 Blomfield Street, appearance was important, and externally the building was faced with terracotta with floral motifs, and was provided with an impressive entrance with an inscription over the doorway (Fig 85). The door led to the staircase which was highly decorative and adorned with deeply-coloured glazed wall tiles and cast-iron stair balusters and handrail. The upper floors, which were designed as offices, were the work of Delissa Joseph. The lower levels, which included the Central London Railway booking hall for Tottenham Court Road Station were designed by Harry Bell Measures.

Two lavatories were provided on the fourth floor of this building and are a reminder that internal flushing conveniences were a relatively recent innovation when these offices opened. The first modern public lavatory with flushing toilets had been another innovative feature of the Great Exhibition at Crystal Palace, and in 1852 the toilets had been relocated to Fleet Street on a permanent basis. Many domestic buildings would wait until the early part of the 20th century for their inside WCs.

NO. 2 FISHER STREET, CAMDEN

Within industrial and commercial workplaces the segregation between the shop floor and the offices and administration, between blue-collar and white-collar workers, employer and employee, management and staff, was becoming more pronounced. This separation is clearly visible in the ground floor plan of the former electricity sub-station at No. 2 Fisher Street, Camden (Gazetteer No. 98) (Figs 86–87).

The original building was the first, and perhaps the most important, sub-station established by the Metropolitan Electric Supply Company Ltd (METESCo) to distribute power from its new central generating facility at Acton Lane, Willesden to its customers in the West End. The sub-station was constructed in 1903-4 on land between Fisher Street to the north and Catton Street (formerly Eagle Street) to the south. Attached to west side of the sub-station was a smaller building, which contained offices, a workshop

Fig 86 Map showing the location of No. 2 Fisher Street. Buildings discussed in the text are shown in blue and labelled with their gazetteer numbers

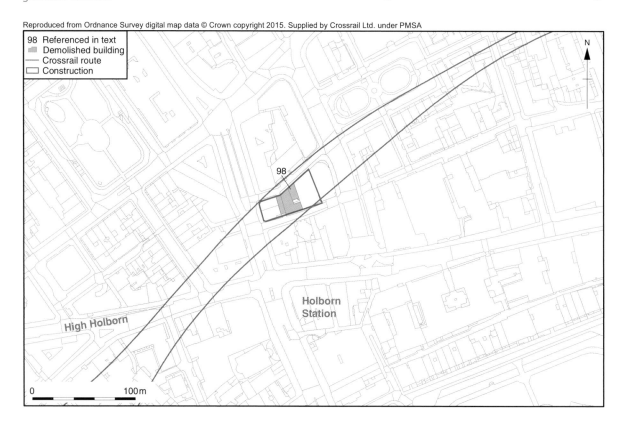

Reproduced from Ordnance Survey digital map data © Crown copyright 2015. Supplied by Crossrail Ltd. under PMSA

98 Referenced in text
Demolished building
Crossrail route
Construction

98

N

Holborn
Station

High Holborn

0   100m

THE CHANGING FACE OF LONDON

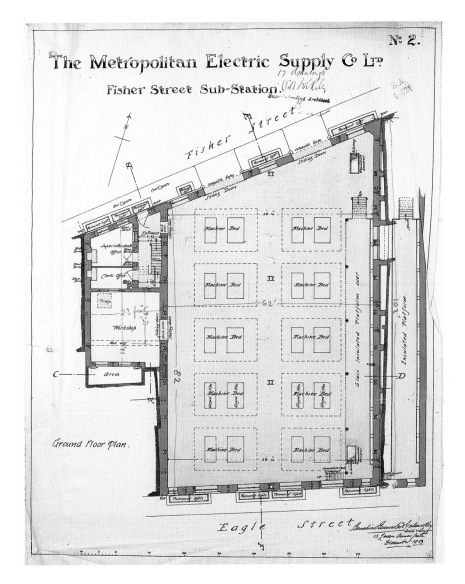

The Metropolitan Electric Supply Co Ltd.

Fisher Street Sub-Station.

N.° 2.

Ground Floor Plan.

Fig 87 Plan of the ground floor of the sub-station at No. 2 Fisher Street, showing the sub-station on the right and the smaller stores and office building on the left. Dec 1903 (London Metropolitan Archives GLC/AR/BR/22/BA/033003)

and stores. This building had four floors and a basement. The sub-station was completely rebuilt in about 1960 with the loss of much of its original Queen Anne-style facade, but the smaller office and stores building at No. 2 Fisher Street survived largely intact and was recorded by Crossrail prior to demolition (Fig 88).

Electricity suppliers tended to build urban sub-stations in a style that would blend in with the surroundings, and a number of celebrated examples were designed for METESCo by Charles Stanley Peach (of Peach & Reilly), who specialised in industrial buildings, including electricity sub-stations. METESCo continued as a separate company until the 1947 Electricity Act nationalised electricity generation and supply, and merged over 600 electrical supply companies into just 12 area boards.

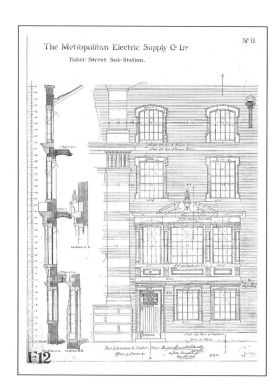

Fig 88 Fisher Street: elevation drawing from 1903 showing the Queen Anne style facade (UK Power Networks)

NO. 65 DAVIES STREET

No. 65 Davies St (Gazetteer No. 55) was a typical example of a purpose-built office constructed in the mid 20th century. It was built in 1948–50 for the British Council, and more recently was the home of the London Institute. The building was demolished to allow the construction of the new western ticket hall for Bond Street Station (Fig 89).

The building was constructed on a frame of steel girders and posts encased in brick or concrete and supporting a series of reinforced concrete decks. The exterior was red brick, except for the ground floor which was faced in rusticated Portland stone cladding. Pale stock brick was used internally. The main elevations comprised large rectangular double-hung

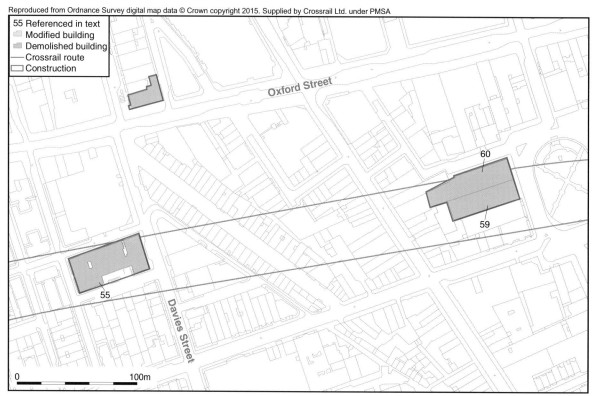

Reproduced from Ordnance Survey digital map data © Crown copyright 2015. Supplied by Crossrail Ltd. under PMSA

55 Referenced in text
Modified building
Demolished building
Crossrail route
Construction

Fig 89 Map showing the location of No. 65 Davies Street. Buildings discussed in the text are shown in blue and labelled with their gazetteer numbers

sash windows, topped by flat arches of rubbed brick with moulded stone sills. The seventh floor was under a mansard style roof (Fig 90).

Fig 90 Exterior view of No. 65 Davies Street

The building occupied the whole area bounded by Davies Street, St. Anselm's Place, Gilbert Street and Weighhouse Street. It was H-shaped in plan, aligned northeast-southwest and comprised north-east and south-west wings with a central link block forming the long axis of the building. On the ground floor, there was a refectory or cafeteria on the north-west side of the central link block. The main entrance with double doors was at the north-east end and the rear entrance at the south-west end of the building. The main entrance gave access via a short flight of stairs and second pair of double doors to a large plain reception area with modern finishes. To the north-west and south-east of the reception were both small and large offices. A central corridor to the south-west ran from the reception passing an open well staircase to the north and a double shaft to the south. The broad concrete staircase had an Art Deco cast iron balustrade, with polished brass-covered handrails, and was illuminated by tall windows. There was a similar staircase and lifts to the upper floors by the rear entrance. The ground floor also had a gallery with windows to the south-east, and there were toilet facilities.

The first floor had a central corridor with original timber and glass double doors at either end, and linked to corridors in each end wing. The corridors had offices to either side, some which had been amalgamated to make larger spaces. The second to sixth floors were similar but workrooms and lecture rooms had been created by amalgamating office spaces. The seventh floor had a large open space with modern suspended ceiling in the central link block. The basement had an open garage space with two vehicle entrances/exits and maintenance workshops. Beneath the south-west block modern offices and computer rooms had been created more recently.

The building was relatively plain, in keeping with the era of post-war austerity in which it had been constructed, but by comparison with more modern office blocks it was of high quality and solidly built to a high standard. The internal office spaces had been modified as the use of the building had changed.

THE MODERN OFFICE BLOCK

It may be that architecture is best appreciated in hindsight and certainly there seems to be greater public appreciation of the value of historic

Fig 91 (left) Caxton House (Numerical Science Ltd)

Fig 92 (right) Cardinal House (Numerical Science Ltd)

Fig 93 Centre Point

buildings compared to more modern structures. Historic England is responsible for the maintenance of the Listed Buildings register and also has the unenviable task of selecting structures which will merit the protection of Listed Building status. The policy for buildings on the register is:

All buildings built before 1700 which survive in anything like their original condition are listed, as are most of those built between 1700 and 1840. Particularly careful selection is required for buildings from the period after 1945. A building has normally to be over 30 years old to be eligible for listing.[9]

Neither Caxton House (Gazetteer No. 100; Fig 91) nor Cardinal House (Gazetteer No. 99; Fig 92) had been listed and there will be few who will mourn the demolition of these stark and functional 1960s office blocks. Both were built over retail outlets and had basement car parking. It was not deemed necessary to record either structure before they were demolished to make way for the construction of the Farringdon West ticket hall shared with Thameslink.

Centre Point (Gazetteer No. 91; Fig 93) is one of the few modern buildings to have been listed and one of the few Listed Buildings affected by Crossrail. It is one of London's iconic structures. Rising to 33 floors and constructed with innovative pre-cast panels hung over a reinforced pre-cast concrete frame, the building epitomises the style which became known as 'Brutalism'. Centre Point embodied the confidence and brashness of the Swinging Sixties. It was constructed as an office block, although incorporating pubs and shops in the lower floors, at a time when there was over-capacity of office space and a housing shortage. It stood empty for many years and came to symbolise the speculative greed of the 1960s.

Despite its innovative design and its notoriety the listing comments that 'the majority of the office, retail and residential interiors lack special interest'. Once more effort and expenditure had been concentrated in the external appearance and the areas used by visitors. Centre Point's external design was impressive, but ultimately proved to be flawed. Its pedestrian subway attracted anti-social activity and the arrangement of its surrounding pavements encouraged pedestrians into the bus lane as they tried to pass the building. With the Crossrail redevelopment of Tottenham Court Road Station the traffic island beneath Centre Point is being redesigned as an open space.

The layout and organisation of the office and the introduction of new technology

The story of the development of the purpose-built office seems to have an underlying theme that 'everything changes, everything stays the same'. Some commentators writing about offices and office work have suggested that the design and layout of offices seems to be more about fashion, cost, and changing ideas of hierarchy, than consideration of the work to be done, or the needs of the employees. The open office plan has been variously adapted with arrangements of cubicles or temporary partitions, and recent high profile experiments with remote working, the 'virtual office' and hot desking have apparently foundered on the rocks of declining productivity.[10]

Certainly the design and appearance of the exterior of Centre Point seems to have been given more consideration than the interior. It has been suggested in the case of Nos 11–12 Blomfield Street that the internal decorative finishes, door cases and stairwells were of high quality and intended to impress and that the external decorative terracottas and the well-appointed staircase to the upper floors at Nos 9–15 Oxford Street served the same purpose. This was hardly new in the later 19th century, for it is clear that East India House, built in the later 18th century, was designed to give an impression of solidity and weight.

Fig 94 The Remington Typewriter (Grace's Guide to British Industrial History)

THE TECHNOLOGY OF THE OFFICE

19th C	Copying by wet chemical process to produce 'blueprints'
Mid 19th C	Morse code and the Electric Telegraph
1858/1866	The Transatlantic Cable providing telegraphic communication between Britain and North America
Late 19th C	The telephone
Early 20th C	The typewriter
1903	The Remington Typewriter – an increasingly common office tool in the early 1900s
1938	Lazlo Biro patents the ballpoint pen – office use becomes common after the Second World War
1951	LEO (Lyons Electronic Office) – The first computer running business applications
1959	The Xerox 914 copying machine
1971	First email sent in USA (The Queen sends the first UK email in 1976)
1976	Inkjet printer
1976	5 inch floppy disc
1979	Wordstar word processing software
1981	Ms-dos partnership between IBM and Microsoft. Operating system licensed and bundled with computer
1981	$3\frac{1}{2}$ inch floppy disc/diskette
1983	Microsoft announce Word and Windows, but not on sale until 1985.
1983	Apple 'Lisa' computer with Graphic User Interface (GUI)
1984	Laserjet printer
1984	Apple Mac with first mouse
1990	World Wide Web
1993	First Graphic User Interface (GUI) web-browser (Mosaic)

It seems that for the average office worker sitting at a desk, or now at a work-station, in an open plan office, the significant changes to the working environment occurred in the Victorian period when architects and engineers radically improved the office worker's quality of life by addressing questions of lighting, access, and waste management and drainage. Since the late 19th century office buildings have proliferated and many are much larger than their 19th-century predecessors, but essentially they serve the same function.

The biggest changes to office working since the beginning of the 19th century have been technological. From the mid 19th century the electric telegraph using Morse code allowed rapid communication over long distances. In the last quarter of the 19th century the telephone system was developed, allowing speech communication over long distances. In the later 20th century innovations both in communications and data storage have appeared one after another seemingly with increasing frequency. The result has been a transformation of office work with regard to speed of communication and methods of data storage and retrieval.

At the same time there has been a massive expansion of the white-collar sector. The consequence of this was that hierarchies of clerks evolved and eventually a career structure for clerks and latterly middle managers emerged as part of this development. Charles Pooter, the comic creation of George and Weedon Grossmith in 'the diary of a nobody', is the epitome of a senior clerk or middle manager, commuting to the City by bus (or rather omnibus).[11]

It is at least arguable that the traditional office environment had reached its zenith in the late 19th or early 20th century and that that biggest change in office working has come about as a result of the development of the computer from the mid 20th century and subsequently the arrival of the desktop computer, and more recently the laptop computer, tablet and smartphone.

These machines are beginning to revolutionise office working. In the 21st century the focus now seems to be on developing new ways of manipulating, enhancing, sharing and storing data rather than seeking further productivity through the ergonomics of office design. In the 20th century there had been aspirations towards further improvements of the working environment such as Norman Foster's Willis Building in Ipswich which incorporated a gym and swimming pool for the workers, although these have subsequently closed. In the 21st century there are certainly some companies, often those working in more creative areas such as software development, that encourage a more relaxed office environment.

NOTES

1   http://www.crossrail.co.uk/benefits/crossrail-in-numbers 15/01/2014

2   Haigh 2012. Recently there has been an entertaining Radio 4 series *History of Office Life*, by Lucy Kellaway of the Financial Times. There is also a museum of the office: http://www.officemuseum.com/.

3   Based on Census Reports for England and Wales on the Vision of Britain website (URL: http://www.visionofbritain,org.uk/

4   Baladouni 1990, 23

5   Dickens, Sketches by 'Boz', *Illustrative of Every-day Life and Every-day People*, 1836, Characters, Chapter 1: Thoughts about people.

6   http://www.visionofbritain.org.uk/data_cube_page.jsp?data_theme=T_POP&data_cube=N_TOT_POP&u_id=10097836&c_id=10001043&add=N

7   Eg: Metropolitan Local Management Act 1855; The Public Health Act 1848/1875; The National Education Act 1870.

8   Turvey 1993, 147-164; *The Engineer*, May 18th, 1894, 416.

9   http://www.english-heritage.org.uk/caring/listing/listed-buildings

10 Ross Gittins on 'Hot-desking': http://www.smh.com.au/business/how-hotdesking-offices-can-wreck-productivity-20131229-301lh.html [accessed 15/10/2014]; Lucy Kellaway, 'Deskspace: scribes, Dickens and the latest chapter in the story of desks', FT.com, 19 August 2015. http://www.ft.com/cms/s/0/a615081a-39ed-11e5-bbd1-b37bc06f590c.html#axzz3mZZkxCbG [accessed 23/09/2015]; Lucy Kellaway, 'Lucy Kellaway's History of Office Life', FT.com, 20 July 2013: http://www.ft.com/cms/s/2/ea605bd2-ed32-11e2-ad6e-00144febdc0.html [accessed 29/09/2015]

11 George and Weedon Grossmith, *The Diary of a Nobody,* 1892

LONDON AT LEISURE

'I have newly taken a solemne oath about abstaining from plays and wine, which I am resolved to keep according to the letter of the oath, which I keepe by me.'
So wrote London's famous diarist, Samuel Pepys, on New Year's Eve 1661.[1] He saw *The Spanish Curate* the very next day, and was drinking again within the month. In this one episode we see revealed London's enduring power to divert all but the strongest of wills.

This chapter considers examples of two types of building with which Pepys was inveterately familiar – the theatre (in the guise of its brash American cousin the cinema) and the tavern. Of course, both types have evolved, as has London, which has swelled far beyond the reaches of Pepys's city. In fact, in his time much of the Soho area in which three of the buildings discussed here were to be found was still fields, whilst the area of Canning Town where the fourth building was situated remained marshland until the 1850s.

The public house

Pepys would have found much that was familiar in the public house of the 1870s. Indeed, in places like The Cock in Fleet Street, he could have drunk in the very building he had frequented. But by the 1880s the public house was changing. A succession of new or amended licensing laws had begun to restrict the availability of licenses to sell alcohol, and a scramble for licensed property ensued.[2] Public houses rapidly became investment commodities, particularly to the London brewers who moved swiftly to consolidate and expand their tied estates, or to the publicans who 'increasingly made their profit not so much from the sale of drinks . . . [as] the resale of the building fabric'.[3] The value of pubs soared, fanned by the publication in 1899 of a Royal Commission report which recommended a large reduction in the number of outlets.[4] The better class of establishment was particularly attractive because it was seen as being less vulnerable to any future legislation to close down pubs.[5]

The promise of an almost guaranteed rise in value encouraged many to rebuild or improve their pubs. This trend may have motivated a Mr Sumpton in 1899 to instruct his architect, W T Farthing, to design a replacement for The Green Man and French Horn, a public house on the corner of Dean Street and Fareham Street in Soho (Fig 1 and Fig 95).[6] If so, his timing was unfortunate. The same year, at the very height of the

The Greenman or French Horn
Dean Street Oxford Street
Plans Elevations &c of Proposed New Premises
for Mr W. Sumpton

Nº 5.

Front Elevation

Fig 95 W T Farthing's design for the replacement of The Green Man and French Horn, Dean Street, property, 1899; front elevation (London Metropolitan Archives, GLC-AR-BR-22-BA-014832)

High Victorian pub building boom, the London bubble burst and the prices of licensed property collapsed.

Sumpton evidently persisted, because the replacement was built, in the process being renamed The Bath House (Gazetteer No. 77) (Fig 96). Farthing designed the building in the Neo-Renaissance style that had grown popular as a means of countering the attractions offered by the growth in organised sporting events, theatres and music halls. He was helped by the pub's location – the corner site offered daylight and custom from two sides, and made it easy to have multiple entrances. Farthing added a fashionable projecting turret to the corner and surmounted it with a copper-sheathed dome. His shop-style windows were divided by granite pilasters with 'T' shaped capitals and dome-shaped roundels – all traditional fare to the pub architect. Above these he detailed a plain panelled frieze and cornice which contained smaller panels of gilded floral designs. The Dean Street elevation had a rather splendid curved bay window with a highly decorative timber surround and scalloped moulded base, and flanking

Fig 96 The Bath House,
Dean Street, as recorded
for Crossrail in 2010 prior
to demolition

angled windows. Generally, however, the windows were mullioned, with four or six lights and stone sills and surrounds. He chose decorative mosaic lettering in an Art Nouveau script for the name signs (Fig 97).

The Bath House had three entrances, each leading into one or more compartments. Internal geography like this was, as Brandwood et al have pointed out, a defining characteristic of pub planning as it developed in the 19th century, reaching its apogee in the 1880s when the trend was for multiple small bars and snugs.[7] By the turn of the century, the number of individual areas was being trimmed, as publicans learnt the attendant difficulties that proliferation had brought. Bars were becoming larger again, and the saloon, 'the decorative and financial apotheosis of the Victorian pub', had been born.[8] Farthing's complement of rooms was entirely in keeping with this latest trend.

The division of space reflected the Victorian propensity for separating people by class and gender, and made it easier for the publican to justify higher prices. A public bar always occupied the most prominent part of the

Fig 97 A variety of
fonts greeted The Bath
House's customers

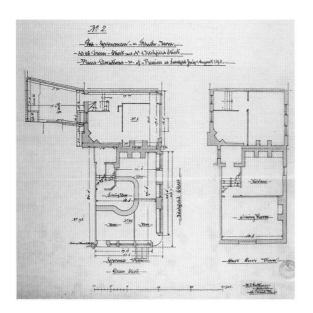
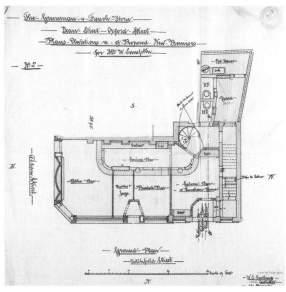

Fig 98 Towards the end
of the 19th century
ground-floor arrange-
ments in pubs started to
change: (left) The floor
plan of The Green Man
and French Horn in 1898;
(right) The floor plan of its
1899 replacement

building beside the busiest thoroughfare – here it was the north–eastern corner where it could be seen from both streets (Fig 98). The deep windows gave it the appearance of a shop and, although this bar, like all public bars, was the cheapest, lowest status room in the establishment, the architectural detailing Farthing provided, especially in the bay window and to the doorway beneath the turret, suggests that even here Sumpton did not wish (or did not think he could afford) to cut costs.

Beside the public bar was a small compartment accessed by a door on Fareham Street, above which a gilded sign read 'Wines and Spirits'. Farthing marked this room on his plans as 'Bottles and Jugs', and it was from here that off-sales were made. This room shared its lobby entrance with the private bar, another feature of the Victorian pub. In practice, it generally denoted no more than a room where the regulars could congregate away from strangers, and it need not necessarily have been furnished to any better standard than the public bar. However, fifty years later, Basil Oliver observed that many of these had become so popular with the 'fair sex' that they had 'virtually become, in many houses, a Women's Bar'.[9]

Beside the private bar, and furthest from the hustle and bustle of Dean Street, lay the 'Saloon Bar and Luncheon Room', undoubtedly the plushest of all, and accessed by its own large, ornate doorway with flanking pilasters supporting an arched head with a broken pediment and a large keystone. Fittingly, this is the only room where Farthing showed seating, possibly because this was the only room where this convenience rose above the simple wooden bench. It was here that artisans, clerks and shopkeepers might drink.

To the right of the Saloon Bar lobby was an arched entrance over a short flight of steps and a landing, beyond which lay the stairs to the first-floor club room. The publican's generous accommodation on the uppermost floors was accessed via a separate flight of stairs behind the public stairs. There were five bedrooms in all, and it is probable that most were let to boarders. The club (or function) room was another common feature of Victorian pubs, and 'a reminder of how much the pub functioned as a social centre, and the headquarters for a huge range of clubs, before the First World War'.[10] Farthing furnished The Bath House's club room with its own lavatory and sink, and up to its demolition in 2010 it retained parts of his ornate cornice detailing (Fig 99).

Fig 99 An original cornice in The Bath House's club room

In another characteristic of the Victorian pub, each ground-floor area (and the first-floor club room) was served by the same bar, here ranged against the south wall. All areas could therefore be efficiently supervised whilst 'customers [who] had to be segregated from each other . . . still [had] . . . immediate access to the bar'.[11] The introduction of the bar counter had been 'the most revolutionary aspect in the transition from traditional tavern to pub, for it immediately changed the whole relationship of the publican to his customers. He was no longer 'mine host' but one of the nation of shopkeepers'.[12]

The Campaign for Real Ale has noted that 'few pub interiors are the same now, or nearly so, as when they were built, and many that have so far survived are pub interiors at risk from being lost'.[13] Almost all of The Bath House's original fixtures and finishes were long gone, so exactly how the interior was initially decorated is unclear (Fig 100). However, it was almost certainly an expression of the High Victorian frou frou displayed magnificently to this day by the nearby Argyll. This retains its glazed tiles, its monumental shelves and counters of mahogany, and its etched and cut glass mirrors. Mirrors, of course, were encouraged by the authorities in the belief that publicans could keep stricter control if they could see their customers' faces at all times. They also provided company for the solitary customer, and helped to distribute what daylight might filter through London's pea-soupers. Like the Argyll, The Bath House would undoubtedly have been decorated with the embossed wallpapers which had grown in popularity as the methods by which they could be produced cheapened. Frederick Walton's 'Lincrusta' was introduced in 1877, and the 'Anaglypta' and 'Cameoid' processes were patented in 1887 and 1888 respectively.[14] The industrialisation of wallpaper production is a reminder that the great pub building boom of the late 19th century provided many Victorian companies

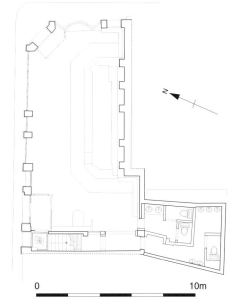

0   10m

Fig 100 The final layout of The Bath House in 2010. The original partitions were long gone

with custom. The window sash pulleys from the upper storeys of The Bath House, for example, were proprietary items from the catalogues of H and T Vaughan of Willenhall in the West Midlands.

If The Bath House's architectural detailing reflected the need for a back-street pub to draw attention to itself The Excelsior, on the junction of busy Charing Cross Road and Oxford Street, needed a design to match its prominent position (167 Charing Cross Road, Gazetteer No. 87; see Fig 1). Built in 1889 to replace the King's Head, which had been on the site since at least 1759, The Excelsior's name and Neo-Renaissance facade were designed to entice the respectable middle class.[15] The ornate archway that led into Falconberg Court was formed from an intricate cast iron overmantle hung from a cosmetic arch; decorative stucco pilasters with anthropomorphic capitals flanked the entrance (Fig 101). To the right was a gently curved bay window on each of the upper three floors, each with columned marble mullions carrying an ornate capital. The bays to either side were narrower; above the top window in all three were head stops, in the Gothic tradition. The roof was masked from view by a semi-circular pediment bearing the date 1889 and mounted by a stone board with carved scrolls and a wreath. The corner to the rear wall of the building was curved, and there were corner windows at each storey (the first-floor window retained its curved panes). Although its architecture no doubt served it well, The Excelsior was outdated and old-fashioned by the time it closed in the 1960s. By 2009, when it was demolished, no internal traces of its former use survived.

Farthing and The Excelsior's unknown architect were no doubt under client instruction to sprinkle their buildings with stardust. As Gorham and Dunnett have put it 'pubs began to aim at being not only unlike their customers' own homes but unlike anybody's home'.[16] This was the West End of London, where wealthy shoppers and businessmen might be attracted by day, and revellers by night. It was a world away from London's docklands, where trade and commerce were the order of the day, and where the third of the pubs considered in this chapter was situated.

When in 1850 George Parker Bidder, Thomas Brassey and Samuel Peto were granted permission to construct Victoria Dock on Plaistow Marshes, the North Woolwich railway line, which followed the curved north bank of the Thames at this point, had to be diverted around the north side of the development.[17] The new loop, which opened in 1855, was provided with a station at the dock's Custom House. For some years the station looked out over marshland to the north, but by 1862 The Freemasons Tavern (Gazetteer No. 137) had been established at the corner of North Woolwich Road and Dirty Lane, as Victoria Dock Road and Freemasons Road were then called (Figs 102-3).[18]

Fig 101 The ornate carriage entrance between The Astoria and The Excelsior

THE CHANGING FACE OF LONDON

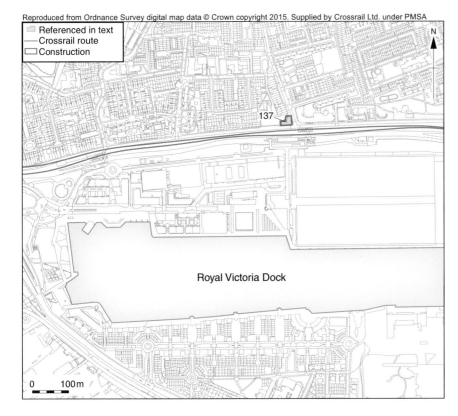

Referenced in text
—Crossrail route
☐ Construction

137

Royal Victoria Dock

N

0   100m

Fig 102 Map showing the location of The Barge in relation to Royal Victoria Dock in Canning Town

The architect evidently had little use for either the decorative excesses of the West End, or the 'old tavern' style that Vigers and Wagstaffe were to use for the nearby Ship in 1880.[19] The facade was sober, regimented and rather restrained. It was, in truth, old-fashioned when compared, for example, with the elaborate Commercial in Tower Hamlets, built only three years later. The name reflected the development 'of the modern masonic brotherhood which . . . often held lodge meetings in taverns and inns',[20] and suggests the intention was to appeal to the middle classes who had business at the docks.

Fig 103 The Barge – formerly The Freemasons Tavern 2009

Perhaps it was only later, as the tide began to turn against the respectable being seen in such establishments, that the pub started catering for the working classes who came to form the vast majority of Canning Town's population. Certainly by 1877 there is evidence that dock workers were drinking there – in June of that year a Richard Scott 'who had worked many years at the docks' was found not guilty of using counterfeit coins to buy drink.[21]

In its final form, The Freemasons Tavern was an L-shaped building of two ranges, the earlier of which, on Victoria Dock Road, was formed from a three-storey corner block beside a two-storey section. The two-storey part had a moulded cornice and low rise parapet, both rendered, above floor-to-ceiling windows that overlooked the dock and continued into the three-storey section. Between 1899 and 1912, when the building was captured by a photographer following events during a dock strike, a two-storey range was added to the Freemasons Road frontage. Its centrepiece was a fine Art Nouveau-style entrance lobby with an ornate wrought iron over-mantle that carried the words 'Saloon Bar' (Fig 104). To the north of the entrance was a contemporary single-storey addition with a decorative plasterwork relief and a key-stoned pediment. The cascading effect created by adding a one-storey block to blocks of two and three storeys was an odd one.

The rounded corner of the building's upper storeys had a panel on which the sign of the public house would have been displayed. In the 1912 photograph there is also a rounded, signwritten panel beneath the frieze, in a place where one would normally expect a doorway; perhaps this had replaced an entrance when the ornate doorway to the north had been added.

Inevitably, London's docks were heavily targeted during the Second World War, and in September 1940 Custom House Station was hit by a high-explosive bomb. The Freemasons Tavern survived the attack, but the very evident, and rather functional, post-war rebuilding of the second floor of the corner block suggests that it was probably quite extensively damaged. In 1951 the pub was re-named The Barge, probably for no reason other than whim, but perhaps as one result of a powerful wave of local post-war activism that would have frowned on the class connotations invoked by the original name.

The cinema

Pepys began his diary as the eighteen-year Puritan ban on the performance of plays in London was being relaxed. The new buildings that emerged were no longer the open theatres in the round of Shakespeare's day, but indoor halls that allowed the development of the scenic stage and the proscenium arch. This model proved highly durable, and was still being applied to theatres over two hundred years later when, in the 1880s, a great period of theatre building began. The theatre's bawdier cousin, the music hall, also saw tremendous growth during the late 19th century so that by 1875 there were 335 music halls in Greater London alone.[22] By the 1920s, however, a new form of entertainment was threatening to eclipse both. Cinema had evolved in the theatre, but technological advances quickly made it a hugely successful industry in its own right. London's first purpose-built 'super' cinema – the Shepherd's Bush Pavilion – opened in 1923. Five years later, the 'talkies' arrived in London, coinciding almost exactly with the submission of plans by Edward Albert Stone to convert Crosse & Blackwell's pickle warehouse on Charing Cross Road into a cinema and dance hall.[23] The Astoria cinema (Gazetteer No. 84; Figs 105-6) opened its doors in January 1927 with a showing of Ivor Novello's *Triumph of the Rat*.

Fig 105 The corner of Charing Cross Road and Oxford Street. The Excelsior is dwarfed by The Astoria

Cinema lent itself to being shown in re-used buildings – in Norfolk, for example, only half of the county's seventy cinemas were purpose-built.[24] Inside the gutted brick shell of Roumieu and Aitchison's 1893 warehouse Griggs & Sons, Stone's favoured building contractors, installed a Roman proscenium theatre to a design by Marc-Henri and Laverdet.[25] Portland cement stucco was used to reface the Charing Cross Road facade in the Neo-Renaissance style, and a turret was added to the top of the south-eastern corner to reflect a similar feature on the building opposite. The ground floor was raised, and a tanked double-depth basement, an octagonal central space surrounded by a gallery, was sunk to create a dance hall big enough to accommodate 1,000 people. A circular foyer for the cinema was created beyond a large recess at the corner of Charing Cross Road and Sutton Street; the dance hall was accessed from 165 Charing Cross Road. A Compton theatre organ was ordered, a panelled barrel-vault ceiling installed, and a cafe 'in which teas and light refreshments are served' appeared in the foyer area. Behind these fancy trimmings, however, the warehouse was still very much in evidence - external plain red brick walls (which Stone's engineer, Major Bell, reinforced with an internal steel frame), concrete beams and large window openings remained in evidence on parts of the building away from the Charing Cross Road facade.

An issue of *The Builder* in 1927 had this to say: 'The vestibule, 25ft wide, has vari-coloured marble columns flanked by gold and white decorations. The proscenium which is flanked by Doric columns, with a grill on each

Fig 106 The Astoria in 2006 (Matthew Lloyd: Arthur Lloyd http://www.arthurlloyd.co.uk)

side concealing the organ, has a richly moulded opening 44ft wide, and the stage is of a depth capable of accommodating the most elaborate style settings'. The article noted approvingly that 'the theatre provides accommodation for 2,000 persons, all with a clear view of the stage'.[26]

Like an evening in The Bath House, a night at the pictures was to be a 'glittering refuge from the drudgery of everyday life'.[27] The list of sub-contractors in the article in *The Builder* provides ample illustration of how Stone set out to achieve this. Carpet Trades Ltd from Kidderminster provided the carpets, Plastering Ltd the external imitation stone renderings, Fenning & Co Ltd the marble work and Jeffrey Ltd the plenum-inducted heating and ventilation system.[28] Clark and Fenn, a contractor from Clapham who were (and still are) a market leader in solid and fibrous plasterwork, made and installed the cinema decoration.[29] 'Every seat in the house', noted *The Builder*, 'is of the new 'tub' style, giving ample knee and elbow room' and 'atmospheric lighting will form one of the presentation features'.[30] Recent improvement in the safety of public theatres was illustrated by the provision of sprinklers by Automatic Sprinkler Co.

The following year, the cinema was acquired by Gaumont Theatres. Ownership changed again in 1931, and in 1948 the Rank Organisation assumed control. In 1957 it was modernised, at which time the seating capacity was reduced to 1,357. In 1964 it hosted the Royal World Premiere of *The Fall of the Roman Empire*, being specially redecorated in a Roman style for the event. The cinema closed in October 1968 to allow a new, plainer auditorium to be installed, with seating capacity reduced again, to 1,121. It was at this time that most of the plasterwork, the inner columns from the proscenium, part of the front of the balcony, the domed ceiling and the original 'Chocolate Store' were lost. The cinema finally closed in 1976, and the building thereafter operated fitfully as a theatre until 1985 when it became a live music venue and nightclub. In January 2009 the building closed its doors for the last time, and demolition to make way for Crossrail's new Tottenham Court Road Station followed shortly afterwards. Plans have been approved for a replacement theatre to be built on the same site.

ACKNOWLEDGEMENTS

The section on the Astoria draws heavily on the work of Ian Grundy and Ken Roe in the website www.cinematreasures.org, and Matthew Lloyd on his website www.arthurlloyd.co.uk.

NOTES

1   Latham and Matthews 1970, 242
2   Brandwood *et al.* 2011, 38-39

3   Elwall 1983, 12

4   Spiller 1972, 92

5   Ball, M and Sunderland, D, 2001, *An Economic History of London 1800–1914*, Routledge, 150

6   This establishment, as The Green Man, may have dated back to the first major redevelopment of Dean Street in 1734; 1899 Architect papers and plans for 96 Dean Street (LMA ref:GLC/AR/BR/22/BA/014832); Westminster Public Library record 0152/016; 'Dean Street Area: Portland Estate, Dean Street', in Survey of London: Volumes 33 and 34, *St Anne Soho*, ed. F H W Sheppard (London, 1966), pp. 128–141 https://www.british-history.ac.uk/survey-london/vols33-4/pp128-141 [accessed 26 September 2015].

7   Brandwood *et al.* 2011, 70

8   Elwall 1983, 13

9   Oliver 1947, 33

10 Brandwood *et al.* 2011, 67

11 Gorham and Dunnett 1950, 26

12 Elwall 1983, 6

13 www.heritagepubs.org.uk, accessed 18 December 2013

14 Gorham and Dunnett 1950, 93

15 'Shaftesbury Avenue and Charing Cross Road', in Survey of London: Volumes 33 and 34, *St Anne Soho*, ed. F H W Sheppard (London, 1966), pp. 296–312 https://www.british-history.ac.uk/survey-london/vols33-4/pp296-312 [accessed 26 September 2015].

16 Gorham and Dunnett 1950, 26

17 Greeves 1980, 9

18 1869 1:1,056 scale Town Plan. The 1850 Town Plan shows that this lane pre-dated any development in the area.

19 Elwall 1983, 28

20 Cox 1994, 30

21 *Old Bailey Proceedings Online* (www.oldbaileyonline.org, version 7.0, 28 February 2014), June 1877, trial of RICHARD SCOTT (32) (t18770625-578)

22 A comprehensive list of London's music halls appears in Howard 1970

23 Stone became the 'house' architect for the Astoria cinema chain, and also drew up plans for Astorias in Brighton, Brixton, Streatham, Finsbury Park and the Old Kent Road in London. The 19th-century history and development of Crosse & Blackwell in Soho is detailed in Jeffries et al forthcoming and Shelley, A, 'The industries of west London' in Brown, R with Shelley, A and Stafford, E, *The Development of West London*, Crossrail Publication Series.

24 Peart 1996, v

25 Griggs & Sons also built the Astoria in Brighton (1933)

26 *The Builder* 1927, 198

27 Elwall 1983, 14

28 The air conditioning of theatres was then a very new technology, having been introduced in Alabama, USA in 1917 by Carrier Engineering Corporation. Carrier were at the forefront of manufacturing ventilation systems for cinemas, and whilst it is not known whether their equipment was used for the Astoria on Charing Cross Road, it is likely; the Astoria's cinemas in Streatham and Finsbury Park, built in 1930, both used it (*The Story of Comfort Air Conditioning*, http://www.hevac-heritage.org/electronic_books/comfort_AC/8-CAC2.pdf (accessed 14 February 2014)

29 Like Carrier, Clark and Fenn, as Clark and Fenn Skanska, survive to this day.

30 *The Builder* 1927, 198

CHAPTER 7

CROSSRAIL'S LEGACY: ENHANCING AND CREATING PLACES

Crossrail is contributing to the changing environment and future built heritage of London. As a significant part of its legacy, it will create over three million square feet of new commercial and residential space across twelve sites. Railways unlock the potential for property development and in 2012 GVA Property Consultants were commissioned to look at the broader impact of Crossrail on London's property market. Their conclusion was that property values in the areas around Crossrail's stations would increase by an average of 18% over and above the market rate. It is predicted that this will in turn potentially accelerate or unlock the development of some 57,000 new homes and a further 3.25 million square metres of offices and shops – equivalent to a town the size of Ipswich.

As a project with significant public sector funding, Crossrail has always sought to deliver more than simply a railway. One of the project's major contributions will be its role as a catalyst for regeneration. In the same way that its Victorian predecessors sought to extend the influence of their stations beyond the confines of railway land, Crossrail's ambitious approach will bequeath an intellectual blueprint for future infrastructure projects and a physical legacy of high quality over-station developments and public spaces. These will add value to the stations, make the property developments more marketable, and help passengers easily navigate their way to and from the stations.

The Metropolitan Railway was the first to realise fully the development opportunities that spring from railway construction. By the end of the First World War they had formed their own property company to promote the vision of 'Metroland', new houses in a suburban countryside connected to the metropolis by a fast rail link. Crossrail aims to ensure that people's experience of the railway does not end at the point of entering or exiting the ticket gate, but continues on into the surrounding environment, buildings and public spaces.

Taking a different approach

Although Crossrail will not be fully operational until 2019, its impact on the property market can already being seen in the investment decisions of some of the biggest property development companies such as Land Securities, Canary Wharf Group, Derwent London and Great Portland Estates. Partners have also been identified for Crossrail's own development programme.

Crossrail's ambition is to deliver an integrated design for its stations, over-station developments and public space improvements and, as a result, significant work has been devoted to the early planning, design and consultation periods. The partner selection process focused on developers who share a vision for providing high-quality buildings set in the best possible surroundings.

To be successful, developers will also have to demonstrate an understanding of the challenges of railway engineering and the needs and aspirations of the communities in which the buildings will sit. Their architects must be capable of providing quality commercial buildings with a long-term use. Local authorities have been actively engaged from the outset and all Crossrail developments and urban realm designs have been reviewed by the Commission for Architecture and the Built Environment (CABE) to ensure Crossrail's ambitions were being realised.

Fig 107 Crossrail's new Canary Wharf Station, May 2014

High-quality developments demand that all parties seek to exceed the already exacting requirements of Crossrail's project sponsors and the Crossrail Act. Masterplans take in a much wider area than is strictly necessary, and emerge only after the demands of pedestrian movement into and from Crossrail stations have been mapped and understood. Paying for such extensive improvements and upgrades to the wider urban realm means looking for further funding. By working with local authorities and other developers to raise additional funds, it is hoped that a further £60 million can be realised to create a total budget of £90 million, perhaps the single biggest investment in London's urban realm for generations.

All of Crossrail's new buildings have faced design challenges, not least when they are to be sited in heritage-sensitive environments. On occasion it has been necessary to remove historic buildings after they have been carefully recorded. For example, the Astoria theatre at the junction of Tottenham Court

Road and Charing Cross Road. In its place, in addition to the new station, two buildings will be created, one of which will provide London's first new West End theatre in a generation. By removing the Astoria, views of the 18th-century St Patrick's church have been created and an attractive walk through to Soho Square has been made possible. Further improvements will also be made to St Giles Circus, and Tottenham Court Road and Charing Cross Road will be returned to two-way traffic. New crossings and improvements in the type and quality of materials used will also help to maximise regeneration benefits to the wider area.

Crossrail has aspired to add to London's corpus of modern architecture. At Fisher Street, for example, Crossrail has eschewed creating a pastiche copy of the fine buildings that surround the site and has instead worked with the local authority and Historic England to develop an exciting and contrasting building that brings something new and different to the area while not detracting from the current frontage.

The measure of time

Crossrail's below-ground infrastructure is of high quality and deliberately uniform in order to make it easily recognisable. In contrast, the design of the above-ground buildings and urban realm has allowed the opportunity to create buildings that are unique, part of the community they serve and responsive to the character of the area in which they sit (Figs 107-109). The aim has been to create dynamic assets that reflect the history, culture

Fig 108 Crossrail's new Paddington Station: architect's impression showing how the transparent station in Eastbourne Terrace allows a view of the Grade 1 listed Paddington Station

Fig 109 Crossrail's new Tottenham Court Road Station: architect's impression of the over-site development which includes a new theatre

and character of each particular area but which are also functional and commercially viable – a nod to the past with an eye on the future.

Crossrail's success will be judged not just on the quality of its rail service, but on the whole experience. The innovative approach to property and urban development will add value to Crossrail's station environments and prove a talking point for years to come.

GAZETTEER

This section offers further details of the buildings discussed in this book. The entries are drawn from, and use the numbering system of, Crossrail's comprehensive gazetteer of the buildings and structures affected by the project. This master gazetteer may be accessed at www.crossrail.co.uk, as may many of the bibliographic sources cited in this volume.

The Monument Type classifications used are drawn from Historic England's Monument Type Thesaurus. The Site Code has been provided by the Museum of London Archaeological Archive.

55: 65 Davies Street, London W1

65 Davies Street, Davies Street elevation.
Facing south-west 2010

Monument type	CL Unassigned, NT Office, CL Education, BT University
Address	65 Davies Street, Mayfair, London W1K 5DA
NGR	528520, 181009
Local Planning Authority	Westminster City Council
Date built	1950
Recording note	Recorded in 2010 in advance of demolition to facilitate construction of Crossrail's Bond Street Station western ticket hall
Architect	Howard, Souster and Partners
Builder/Manufacturer	Not known
Field events	2010, EH Level 2 NLBH record, Wessex Archaeology
Bibliography and sources	Wessex Archaeology, 2010, *65 Davies Street, Bond Street Station, western ticket hall, Historic Building Recording*, C132-XRL-T1-RGN-CRG03-50002
	Wessex Archaeology, 2010, *Crossrail Bond Street Station, 65 Davies Street, Non Listed Built Heritage Recording, Interim Archaeological Statement*, C257-WSX-T1-RSI-C125_WS086-00001
Site code	CXG10
Archive location	LAARC
Volume references	CRL Series No. 3, p38, 74
Characterisation	Seven-storey office block with basement. Neo-Georgian design. Surviving 1950s features included terrazzo flooring, Art Deco staircases and hardwood veneered doors. From 1950 until the late 20th century it was the headquarters for the British Council and from 1993 it was used by the London Institute (later the University of the Arts London).

59: 18 Hanover Square, City of Westminster, London W1

East facing elevation of 18 Hanover Square

Monument type	CL Unassigned, BT Building, NT Office
Address	18 Hanover Square, London W1X 1HZ
NGR	528849, 181092
Local Planning Authority	Westminster City Council
Date built	1962-4
Recording note	Recorded before demolition in 2011 for Bond Street Station eastern ticket hall
Architect	Ronald Fielding Partnerships
Builder/Manufacturer	Not known
Field events	2005, NLBH gazetteer, Alan Baxter and Associates and Chris Blandford and Associates
Bibliography and sources	Crossrail, 2008, *Bond Street Station, Site Specific Archaeological Detailed Desk Based Assessment*, CR-XRL-T1-RGN-CRG03-50001
	Alan Baxter (and Associates) and Chris Blandford Associates, 2006, *Assessment of Impacts on Heritage and Landscape, Technical Report, Volume 3 of 6*, 1E0316-G0E00-00001
Site code	Not assigned for building recording, Technical report only
Archive location	LAARC
Volume reference	p38
Characterisation	6 storey office building with a basement that was 3 bays wide on Hanover Square and 8 bays long on Tenterden Street. Each bay had 4 windows on each level. The building had a steel-frame construction with concrete cladding to panels and tiled edges with articulation given to the raised parapet.

60: 19 Hanover Square, City of Westminster, London W1

East facing facade of 19 Hanover Square

Monument type	CL Unassigned, BT Building, NT Office
Address	19 Hanover Square, London W1X 1HZ
NGR	528854, 181076
Local Planning Authority	Westminster City Council
Date built	1973
Recording note	Recorded before demolition in 2011 for the eastern ticket hall of Crossrail's Bond Street Station
Architect	Burnet, Tait & Partners
Builder/Manufacturer	Not known
Field events	2005, NLBH gazetteer, Alan Baxter & Associates and Chris Blandford Associates
Bibliography and sources	Crossrail, 2008, Bond Street Station, Site Specific *Archaeological Detailed Desk Based Assessment*, CR-XRL-T1-RGN-CRG03-50001
	Alan Baxter & Associates and Chris Blandford Associates, 2006, *Assessment of Impacts on Heritage and Landscape, Technical Report*, Volume 3 of 6, 1E0316-G0E00-00001
Site code	Not assigned for building recording, Technical report only
Archive location	LAARC
Volume reference	p38
Characterisation	19 Hanover Square (adjoined Grade II★ listed 20 Hanover Square). This office building had six storeys over a basement and a leaded mansard roof. It had a steel frame construction with stone cladding to the armature of the building and possible marble cladding to window aprons. Each storey had ten windows that were serried and framed by abstracted pilasters.

65: 5a Great Chapel Street, London W1

 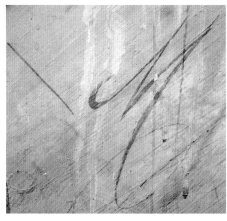

Detail of early 18th-century stairs (left); a signature which lay hidden beneath a covering board on the uppermost side rail (right) 2010

Monument type	CL Domestic, BT House; CL Commercial, (possible BT Warehouse)
Address	5a Great Chapel Street, Soho, London W1F 8FL
NGR	529550, 181287
Local Planning Authority	Westminster City Council
Date built	House: later 19th-century; staircase: early 18th-century
Recording note	Recorded in advance of demolition in 2010 to facilitate construction of Crossrail's Tottenham Court Road Station western ticket hall
Architect	Not known
Builder/Manufacturer	Not known
Field events	2010, EH Level 1 NLBH record, Oxford Archaeology/Ramboll
Bibliography and sources	Crossrail 2010, *Design Package C134. Tottenham Court Road Station. Addendum to WSI: Building Recording at 5a Great Chapel Street,* C134-OVE-T1-RGN-N105-00021
	Oxford Archaeology/Ramboll 2013, *Building recording at Tottenham Court Road Station. Event Code XRY10, Archaeological Interim Statement,* C254-OXF-W-RGN-N105-50004 Rev 2
Site code	XRY10
Archive location	LAARC
Volume reference	p19
Characterisation	Four-storey building with a similar layout on each floor. The 1730s staircase pre-dated the building, suggesting re-use. A hatch on each floor allowed for vertical movement, possibly of goods. During demolition floral wallpaper was exposed by the removal of later abutting partitions at ground, first and second floor levels.

68: 9 Great Chapel Street / 4 Fareham Street, London W1

General view of 9 Great Chapel Street, facing north-east 2004

Monument type	CL Commercial, BT Shop
Address	9 Great Chapel Street, London W1F 8FH
NGR	529558, 181260
Local Planning Authority	Westminster City Council
Date built	Late 19th century
Recording note	Recorded in 2010 in advance of demolition to facilitate construction of Crossrail's Tottenham Court Road Station western ticket hall
Architect	Not known
Builder/Manufacturer	Not known
Field events	2010, EH Level 1 NLBH record, Wessex Archaeology
Bibliography and sources	Wessex Archaeology, 2010, *Tottenham Court Station, Soho, London. Non-Listed Built Heritage Recording*, C134-XRL-T1-RGN-CRG03-50001
	Wessex Archaeology, 2010, *Tottenham Court Road Station, Soho, London. Interim Statement – Historic Building Recording, South Block*, C262-XRL-T1-RGN-CRG03-50004
Site code	XRY10
Archive location	LAARC
Volume reference	p33
Characterisation	Four-storey building with a basement located on the corner of Great Chapel Street and Fareham Street. 'Norman Shaw' style with decorative features such as three white horizontal string courses, friezes, a brick parapet and brick gables on the third floor. Shopfront at ground floor level with replacement windows. A few interior historic features remained such as timber doors and cases, timber cornicing and a staircase with winders.

72: 2-3 Fareham Street, London W1

General view of 2-3 Fareham Street, W1, north-east elevation, looking east 2010

Monument type	CL Commercial, BT Warehouse; CL Industrial, BT Workshop
Address	2-3 Fareham Street, London W1D 3BB
NGR	529568, 181265
Local Planning Authority	Westminster City Council
Date built	Late 19th or early 20th century
Recording note	Recorded in 2010 inadvance of demolition to facilitate construction of Crossrail's Tottenham Court Road Station western ticket hall
Architect	Not known
Builder/Manufacturer	Not known
Field events	2010, EH Level 2 NLBH record, Wessex Archaeology
Bibliography and sources	Wessex Archaeology, 2010, *Crossrail Tottenham Court Station Non-Listed Built Heritage Statement*, C134-XRL-T1-RGN-CRG03-50001
	Wessex Archaeology, 2010, *Tottenham Court Road Station Interim Statement – Historic Building Recording, South Block*, C262-XRL-T1-RGN-CRG03-50004
Site code	XRY10
Archive location	LAARC
Volume reference	p34
Characterisation	Four-storey red brick building with basement. Constructed using timber joists on transverse steel beams. The main facade had three bays with large arched fenestration and altered windows. Each floor had the same single room arrangement. Used by a jewellery case maker in the early 20th century.

77: The Bath House, 96 Dean Street, London W1

The Bath House (left) 2010; signage on the north elevation (right)

Monument type	CL Commercial, BT Public House
Address	96 Dean Street, London W1D 3TD
NGR	529581, 181267
Local Planning Authority	Westminster City Council
Date built	1899
Recording note	Recorded in 2010 in advance of demolition to facilitate construction of Crossrail's Tottenham Court Road Station western ticket hall
Architect	W T Farthing
Builder/Manufacturer	Not known
Field events	2010, EH Level 3 NLBH record, Wessex Archaeology
Bibliography and sources	Wessex Archaeology, 2010, *Design Package C134, Tottenham Court Station, Non-Listed Built Heritage Recording*, C134-XRL-T1-RGN-CRG03-50001
	Oxford Archaeology/Ramboll, 2010, *Building Recording at Tottenham Court Road Station, Archaeological Interim Report*, C254-OXF-W-RGN-N105-50004
Site code	XRY10
Archive location	LAARC
Volume reference	p82
Characterisation	Built for a Mr Sumpton to replace The Green Man and French Horn which had occupied the same plot and, as The Green Man, may have dated back to the first major re-development of Dean Street in 1734.

78: 95 Dean Street, London W1

95 Dean Street, facing south-west 2004

Monument type	CL Commercial, BT Shop; CL Domestic, NT Terraced House
Address	95 Dean Street, London W1D 3TB
NGR	529583,181264
Local Planning Authority	Westminster City Council
Date built	Likely 18th century but extensively rebuilt in the 19th century
Recording note	Recorded in 2010 in advance of demolition for Crossrail's Tottenham Court Road Station western ticket hall
Architect	Not known
Builder/Manufacturer	Not known
Field events	2010, EH Level 1 NLBH record, Wessex Archaeology
Bibliography and sources	Wessex Archaeology, 2010, *Tottenham Court Station, Soho, London. Non-Listed Built Heritage Recording*, C134-XRL-T1-RGN-CRG03-50001
	Wessex Archaeology, 2010, *Tottenham Court Road Station, Soho, London. Interim Statement – Historic Building Recording, South Block*, C262-XRL-T1-RGN-CRG03-50004
Site code	XRY10
Archive location	LAARC
Volume reference	p28
Characterisation	Four-storey building with stock brick frontage and highly decorative pedimented window surrounds at first-floor level. This building may have been labelled as 70 Dean Street on Horwood's 1792 map (the road was renumbered between 1808-1816). Building altered in the mid 19th century to create a new shopfront with plain pilasters and console-bracketed capitals with a decorative flower boss.

94 Dean Street, facing south-west (left) 2003; closed string staircase (right)

Monument type	CL Commercial, BT Shop; CL Domestic, NT Terraced House
Address	94 Dean Street, London W1D 3TA
NGR	529586, 181258
Local Planning Authority	Westminster City Council
Date built	Early 18th century; extensive alterations 19th century
Recording note	Recorded in 2010 in advance of demolition for Crossrail's Tottenham Court Road Station western ticket hall
Architect	Not known
Builder/Manufacturer	Not known
Field events	2008–2010, EH Level 3 NLBH record, Scott Wilson and Oxford Archaeology/Ramboll
Bibliography and sources	Crossrail, 2008, *Multi-disciplinary consultant works, Package 2, City of Westminster Heritage Agreement, Building Recording of 94 Dean Street*, CRL1-XRL-T-QCP-N105-00044
	Crossrail, 2008, *Multi-disciplinary consultant works, Package 2, City of Westminster Heritage Agreement, Method Statements for 94 Dean Street and Bollards on Fareham Street*, CRL1-XRL-T-QCP-N105-00045
	Oxford Archaeology/Ramboll, 2010, *Building recording at 94 Dean Street, Final Fieldwork Report*, C254-OXF-T1-RGN-CRG03-50148
Site code	XRY10
Archive location	LAARC
Volume reference	p14
Characterisation	Former Grade II listing (list no. 1290540). Previously of four-storeys plus basement, two bays wide. Extensive alterations in the 19th century, including a plastered shop front. Although listed in 1978 most historic fittings, apart from its closed string staircase, appeared to have been stripped away by the time of the 2008 survey.

80: 9 Diadem Court, London W1

General view of 9 Diadem Court (left) 2010; detail of fireplace (right)

Monument type	CL Domestic; BT Dwelling
Address	9 Diadem Court, London W1D 3EG
NGR	529589, 181249
Local Planning Authority	Westminster City Council
Date built	Mid-19th century
Recording note	Recorded in 2010 in advance of demolition for Crossrail's Tottenham Court Road Station western ticket hall
Architect	Not known
Builder/Manufacturer	Not known
Field events	2010, EH Level 1 NLBH record, Wessex Archaeology
Bibliography and sources	Wessex Archaeology, 2010, *Crossrail Tottenham Court Station Non-Listed Built Heritage Statement*, C134-XRL-T1-RGN-CRG03-50001;
	Wessex Archaeology, 2010, *Tottenham Court Road Station Interim Statement – Historic Building Recording, South Block*, C262-XRL-T1-RGN-CRG03-50004
Site code	XRY10
Archive location	LAARC
Volume reference	p18
Characterisation	Four-storey, London stock brick building with principal elevation on Diadem Court. Ground floor doorway and adjacent large window both had segmental brick arched heads. Each floor had one large room with an adjacent WC and smaller room to the rear. Victorian staircase with a dado rail and skirting, sash windows and cast iron fireplaces.

General view of 93 Dean Street 2004. Facing north-west

Monument type	CL Domestic, BT Dwelling; CL Commercial, BT Shop, CL Commercial, NT Coffee Bar; CL Recreational, NT Discotheque
Address	93 Dean Street, London W1D 3RQ
NGR	529592, 181251
Local Planning Authority	Westminster City Council
Date built	Mid-19th century
Recoding note	Recorded in 2010 in advance of demolition for Crossrail's Tottenham Court Road Station western ticket hall
Architect	Not known
Builder/Manufacturer	Not known
Field events	2010, EH Level 1 NLBH record, Wessex Archaeology
Bibliography and sources	Wessex Archaeology, 2010, *Tottenham Court Station, Soho, London. Non-Listed Built Heritage Recording*, C134-XRL-T1-RGN-CRG03-50001;
	Wessex Archaeology, 2010, *Tottenham Court Road Station, Soho, London. Interim Statement – Historic Building Recording, South Block*, C262-XRL-T1-RGN-CRG03-50004
	Les Enfants Terribles, www.lesenfantsterribles.adrianstern.com
Site code	XRY10
Archive location	LAARC
Volume references	p17, 32
Characterisation	Four-storey building in London stock brick. Chamfered bay on south-east corner with two bays either side (two on each street). Ground floor used as a shop, latterly a café and bar.

83: Oxford House, 9-15 Oxford Street, London W1

9-15 Oxford Street, facing south 2009

Monument type	CL Transport, NT Underground Railway Station, CL Commercial, NT Shopping Parade; CL Commercial, BT Commercial Office
Address	Oxford House, 9-15 Oxford Street, London W1D 2DG
NGR	529789,181361
Local Planning Authority	Westminster City Council
Date built	Late 1890s
Recording note	Recorded in 2008 in advance of part demolition to faciliate construction of Crossrail's Tottenham Court Road Station eastern ticket hall
Architect	Station (ground floor and basement): Harry Bell Measures; Upper storeys: Delissa Joseph
Builder/Manufacturer	Not known
Original railway company	Central London Railway
Field events	2008-2009, EH Level 1 NLBH record, MOLA
Bibliography and sources	MOLA, 2009, *Tottenham Court Road Station Upgrade. 1-15 Oxford Street, 157-167 and 138-148 Charing Cross Road, 1-6 Falconberg Court, London WC2*
Site code	GCI08
Archive location	LAARC
Volume reference	p71; CRL Series No.4, p28
Characterisation	CLR's architect Measures designed a string of stations. These were specifically intended to carry upper storeys that had been designed and constructed by others. The parts of the building demolished by Crossrail largely corresponded to Joseph's development.

84: Astoria Theatre, 157-165 Charing Cross Road, London W1

The Astoria Theatre, Charing Cross Road in 2006. Facing north-west

Monument type	CL Commercial, BT Warehouse; CL Recreational, BT Cinema
Address	157-165 Charing Cross Road, London W1
NGR	529797, 181316
Local Planning Authority	Westminster City Council
Date built	Warehouse completed 1893; converted to cinema and dance hall 1926-27; theatre and music venue from 1985
Recording note	Recorded in 2008 in advance of demolition to facilitate construction of Crossrail's Tottenham Court Road Station eastern ticket hall
Architect	Warehouse: Roumieu and Aitchison; Cinema and dance hall: Edward Albert Stone
Builder/Manufacturer	Cinema and dance hall: Griggs and Son Limited
Field events	2008-2009, EH Level 3 NLBH record, MOLA
Bibliography and sources	MOLA, 2009, *Tottenham Court Road Station Upgrade. 1-15 Oxford Street, 157-167 and 138-148 Charing Cross Road, 1-6 Falconberg Court, London WC2: Standing Building Survey*;
	The Builder, 4 February 1927, 198-203, in Vol CXXXII Jan to June 1927
Site code	GCI08
Archive location	LAARC
Volume reference	p89
Characterisation	Built as a pickle warehouse for Crosse and Blackwell. In 1927 Stone converted it into a cinema and dance hall (the engineer was Major Bell) for the Astoria chain. After 1948 the cinema became part of the Rank Organisation and was progressively reduced in capacity. The cinema closed in 1976 and in 1985 it became a music venue and nightclub.

1 to 7 Oxford Street, facing south-west 2009

Monument type	CL Commercial; BT Shop; CL Unassigned, BT Office; CL Commercial, Bank (financial)
Address	1-7 Oxford Street, London W1D 2DF
NGR	529805, 181357
Local Planning Authority	Westminster City Council
Date built	Late 1880s
Recording note	Recorded in 2008 in advance of demolition to facilitate construction of Crossrail's Tottenham Court Road Station eastern ticket hall
Architect	T M Houghton
Builder/Manufacturer	Not known
Field events	2008-2009, EH Level 1 NLBH record, MOLA
Bibliography and sources	MOLA, 2009, *Tottenham Court Road Station Upgrade. 1-15 Oxford Street, 157-167 and 138-148 Charing Cross Road, 1-6 Falconberg Court, London WC2*
Site code	GCI08
Archive location	LAARC
Volume reference	p37
Characterisation	Corner site with four distinct premises, each with a basement, ground floor and four upper floors. A red brick building with highly decorative stone window surrounds. The facades of 3 and 5 Oxford Street were refaced with Portland stone, probably in the 1930s, and housed a branch of Barclays Bank.

87: The Excelsior, 167 Charing Cross Road, London WC2

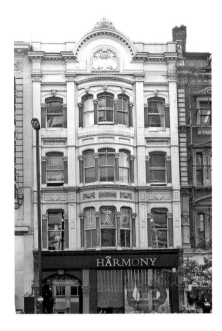

Exterior of 167 Charing Cross Road, facing west 2004

Monument type	CL Commercial, NT Public House; CL Commercial, Shop
Address	167 Charing Cross Road, London WC2H 0EN
NGR	529811, 181334
Local Planning Authority	Westminster City Council
Date built	1889
Recording note	Recorded in 2008 in advance of demolition to facilitate construction of Crossrail's Tottenham Court Road Station eastern ticket hall
Architect	Not known
Builder/Manufacturer	Not known
Field events	2008-2009, EH Level 1 NLBH record, MOLA
Bibliography and sources	MOLA, 2009, *Tottenham Court Road Station Upgrade. 1-15 Oxford Street, 157-167 and 138-148 Charing Cross Road, 1-6 Falconberg Court, London WC2: Standing Building Survey*
Site code	GCI08
Archive location	LAARC
Volume reference	p86
Characterisation	This building replaced the Kings Head, a public house from at least 1759. By the late 1970s the pub was closed and the ground-floor was a Wimpy café.

91: Centre Point plaza, 101-103 Oxford Street, London WC1

Centre Point, facing east (left); Centre Point's plaza (above) 2011

Monument type	CL Gardens Parks and Urban Spaces, Ornamental Pool; CL Gardens Parks and Urban Spaces, NT Public Square; CL Transport, BT Pedestrian Transport Site, NT Subway; CL Water Supply and Drainage; NT Public Convenience; CL Recreational, NT Snooker Hall
Address	Centre Point, 101–103 Oxford Street, London WC1
NGR	529848, 181345
Local Planning Authority	Camden Council
Date built	1963–67
Recording note	Centre Point's plaza and pool, subway, public toilets and snooker club recorded in 2008 before closing for refurbishment or replacement
Architect	Centre Point: Seifert and Partners/George Marsh, Plaza: Jupp Dernbach-Mayen
Builder/Manufacturer	Wimpey Construction
Field events	2008, EH Levels 2 and 3 NLBH record, MOLA
Bibliography and sources	MOLA, 2009, *Centre Point, 101-103 Oxford Street, London WC2. Standing Building Survey*
Site code	GCI08
Archive location	LAARC
Volume reference	p76
Characterisation	Grade II listed (entry 1113172) in 1995.

92: 142 and 146 Charing Cross Road, London WC2

Exterior of 142 and 146 Charing Cross Road, facing east 2009

Monument type	CL Commercial, BT Shop; CL Unassigned, BT Office
Address	142 and 146 Charing Cross Road, London WC2H 0LA
NGR	529853, 181289
Local Planning Authority	Camden Council
Date built	Completed 1888
Recording note	Recorded in 2009 in advance of demolition to facilitate construction of Crossrail's Tottenham Court Road Station eastern ticket hall
Architect	H H Collins
Builder/Manufacturer	Not known
Field events	2008-2009, EH Level 1 NLBH record, MOLA
Bibliography and sources	MOLA, 2009, *Tottenham Court Road Station Upgrade. 1-15 Oxford Street, 157-167 and 138-148 Charing Cross Road, 1-6 Falconberg Court, London WC2.*
Site code	GCI08
Archive location	LAARC
Volume reference	p34
Characterisation	Four-storey building with basement. Ground floor had shops either side of a central port-cochere which gave access to Crown Place Yard.

93: 148 Charing Cross Road, London WC2

148 Charing Cross Road, facing south-east (left); spiral staircase (right) 2009

Monument type	CL Commercial, BT Showroom; CL Commercial; BT Shop; CL Unassigned, BT Office; CL Recreational, NT Nightclub
Address	148 Charing Cross Road, London WC2H 0LB
NGR	529854, 181299
Local Planning Authority	Camden Council
Date built	by 1892
Recording note	Recorded in 2008 in advance of demolition to facilitate construction of Crossrail's Tottenham Court Road Station eastern ticket hall
Architect	Bateman and Bateman, Birmingham
Builder/Manufacturer	Not known
Field events	2008-2009, EH Level 1 NLBH record, MOLA
Bibliography and sources	MOLA, 2009, *Tottenham Court Road Station Upgrade. 1-15 Oxford Street, 157-167 and 138-148 Charing Cross Road, 1-6 Falconberg Court, London WC2*
Site code	GCI08
Archive location	LAARC
Volume reference	p34
Characterisation	Red brick building with stucco facade. First and second floor windows recessed in a great arch; attic storey surmounted by a tall pyramidal roof. The interior had a double-height room with a barrel vaulted ceiling, decorative cornice and a spiral staircase.

94: 138 and 140 Charing Cross Road, London WC2

138-140 Charing Cross Road, facing north east 2009

Monument type	CL Commercial; BT Shop; CL Unassigned, BT Office; CL Commercial, BT Café; CL Commercial, NT Internet Café
Address	138 and 140 Charing Cross Road, London WC2H 0LB
NGR	529857, 181275
Local Planning Authority	Camden Council
Date built	1880s
Recording note	Recorded in 2008 in advance of demolition to facilitate construction of Crossrail's Tottenham Court Road Station eastern ticket hall
Architect	Not known
Builder/Manufacturer	Not known
Field events	2008-2009, EH Level 1 NLBH record, MOLA
Bibliography and sources	MOLA, 2009, *Tottenham Court Road Station Upgrade. 1-15 Oxford Street, 157-167 and 138-148 Charing Cross Road, 1-6 Falconberg Court, London WC2*
Site code	GCI08
Archive location	LAARC
Volume reference	p34
Characterisation	Building in three distinct parts – a three-storey northern part, two storey southern part and a 20th-century three storied addition. Red brick facade with a canted corner that had housed the original shop entrance. In 1915 the entire building was occupied by Francis, Day and Hunter, music publishers, who remained there until the later 20th century.

95: 144 Charing Cross Road, London WC2

Exterior of 144 Charing Cross Road. Facing north-east 2009

Monument type	CL Commercial, BT Showroom; CL Commercial, BT Shop; CL Commercial, NT Commercial Office; Recreational, NT Nightclub
Address	144 Charing Cross Road, London WC2H 0LB
NGR	529865, 181299
Local Planning Authority	Camden Council
Date built	Late 19th century
Recording note	Recorded in 2009 in advance of demolition to facilitate Crossrail's Denmark Place redevelopment
Architect	Not known
Builder/Manufacturer	Not known
Field events	2008-2009, EH Level 1 and 2 NLBH record, MOLA
Bibliography and sources	MOLA, 2009, *Tottenham Court Road Station Upgrade. 1-15 Oxford Street, 157-167 and 138-148 Charing Cross Road, 1-6 Falconberg Court, London WC2*
Site code	GCI08
Archive location	LAARC
Volume reference	p34
Characterisation	Located to the rear of 142–146 Charing Cross Road, on the north side of a yard known as Crown Place and accessed through a covered entrance. The six-storey building had three entrances and a basement to the west and two storeys on its eastern side. Linked internally with 148 Charing Cross Road. It was used as a warehouse in the late 19th and early 20th centuries and housed basket makers W G Scott and Sons. Latterly a nightclub.

98: 2 Fisher Street, London WC1

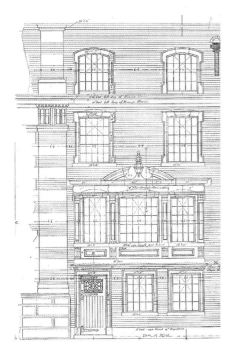

Elevation of 2 Fisher Street in 1903

Monument type	CL Commercial, NT Commercial Office
Address	2 Fisher Street, London WC1A 2RA
NGR	530531, 181614
Local Planning Authority	Camden Council
Date built	1903-1904
Recording note	Recorded in 2010 in advance of demolition to facilitate construction of an emergency access shaft for Crossrail
Architect	Charles Stanley Peach
Builder/Manufacturer	Not known
Field events	2010-2011 NLBH record, Jacobs Engineering UK Limited
Bibliography and sources	Jacobs Engineering UK Limited, 2012, *Fisher Street Shaft Site-Specific Archaeological Written Scheme of Investigation*, C123-JUL-T1-TPL-CR086_SH003_Z-00002 Rev 10.0
Site code	FIS 11
Archive location	LAARC
Volume reference	p72
Characterisation	Three storeys high with a basement. Faced in red brick and Portland stone in an Edwardian/Queen Anne style. The ground floor of the building was used for offices, whilst the first and second floors served as stores for the Metropolitan Electric Supply Company Ltd's nearby electrical sub-station.

99: Cardinal House, 48-53 Cowcross Street, London EC1

Cardinal House, Farringdon Road elevation. Facing south-west 2008

Monument type	CL Commercial, NT Commercial Office; CL Commercial, NT Shopping Parade, CL Transport, NT Underground Car Park
Address	48-53 Cowcross Street, 2a-12 Farringdon Road, London EC1M 3HS
NGR	531563, 181785
Local Planning Authority	Islington Council
Date built	*c.*1960
Recording note	Recorded in 2008. Demolished during 2009 to facilitate construction of Crossrail's Farringdon Station western ticket hall
Architect	Richard Seifert
Builder/Manufacturer	Not known
Field events	None
Bibliography and sources	Crossrail, 2008, *MDC – Work Package 3, Archaeology Detailed Desk Based Assessment, Farringdon Station,* CR-XRL-T1-RGN-CR001-50003
Site code	None
Archive location	LAARC
Volume reference	p76
Characterisation	Twelve-storey office block with outbuildings and street-level shops on Farringdon Road and Cowcross Street. Underground car park accessed via an archway on Cowcross Street.

100: Caxton House, Farringdon Road, London EC1

Caxton House, facing north-east 2003

Monument type	CL Commercial, BT Commercial Office; CL Commercial, BT Shopping Parade; CL Transport, NT Underground Car Park
Address	Caxton House, 2 Farringdon Road, London EC1M 3HN
NGR	531579, 181714
Local Planning Authority	Islington Council
Date built	*c.*1960
Recording note	Recorded in 2008. Demolished during 2009 to facilitate construction of Farringdon Station western ticket hall
Architect	Chapman Taylor Partnership (1979)
Builder/Manufacturer	Not known
Field events	None
Bibliography and sources	Crossrail, 2008, *MDC – Work Package 3, Archaeology Detailed Desk Based Assessment, Farringdon Station*, CR-XRL-T1-RGN-CR001-50003
Site code	None
Archive location	LAARC
Volume reference	p76
Characterisation	Caxton House was an eight-storey office block with an underground car park accessed via a ramp on Cowcross Street. Outbuildings on Farringdon Road and Charterhouse Street contained a parade of shops.

54-64 Charterhouse Street, facing south-east (left) in 2010. Steel decking that had carried the building over tracks and a platform at the eastern end of Smithfield Market's railway lines (right) 2011

Monument type	CL Industrial, NT Workshop; CL Unassigned, BT Depot
Address	54-64 Charterhouse Street, London, EC1M 6JH
NGR	531921, 181836
Local Planning Authority	City of London Corporation
Date built	1930
Recording note	Recorded in 2011 in advance of demolition to facilitate construction of Crossrail's Farringdon Station eastern ticket hall
Architect	S.A.S Yeo
Builder/Manufacturer	Not known
Field events	2011, EH Level 2 NLBH record, Scott Wilson Ltd
Bibliography and sources	Crossrail, 2011, *Farringdon Station: Level II Historic Building Record*, C136-SWN-T1-RGN-M123-50002
	London Metropolitan Archives, Smithfields Goods Station, Armour and Company Limited (1916-1959) GLC/AR/BR/22/BA/043620
Site code	XRU10
Archive location	LAARC
Volume reference	p53
Characterisation	Smithfield House was Armour & Co's meat manufacturing workshop and depot. Constructed using the Hennebique concrete method over a steel lattice deck that carried the building over the railways lines and platforms below. The platform was accessed via 8-9 Hayne Street and 3 Lindsey Street.

108: 3 Lindsey Street, London EC1

3 Lindsey Street, western facade, facing east 2010

Monument type	CL Commercial, NT Butchers Shop; CL Commercial, NT Meat Cellar
Address	3 Lindsey Street, London EC1A 9HP
NGR	531940, 181799
Local Planning Authority	City of London Corporation
Date built	Late 19th century
Recording note	Recorded in 2011 before demolition to facilitate construction of Crossrail's Farringdon Station eastern ticket hall
Architect	Not known
Builder/Manufacturer	Not known
Original railway company	By 1916 basement level linked to GWR office at 4 Lindsey Street and to the railway below
Field events	2011, EH Level 2 NLBH record, Scott Wilson Ltd
Bibliography and sources	Crossrail, 2011, *Farringdon Station: Level II Historic Building Record*, C136-SWN-T1-RGN-M123-50002;London Metropolitan Archives, Smithfields Goods Station, Armour and Company Limited (1916-1959) GLC/AR/BR/22/BA/043620
Site code	XRU10
Archive location	LAARC
Volume reference	p51; CRL Series No.4, p70
Characterisation	Single-storey structure situated over the eastern throat of Smithfield Market's sidings. It was likely to have been used as a meat store throughout its history. Four levels to the building; a platform at rail level, a basement, a ground floor and a mezzanine. Blocked doorways suggest the building could have been linked to the GWR railway offices at 4 Lindsey Street. From 1916 the basement was used as a meat storage area for 8-9 Hayne Street.

109: 8-9 Hayne Street, London EC1

Hayne Street facade facing west 2010

Monument type	CL Commercial, BT Warehouse
Address	8-9 Hayne Street, London EC1A 9HH
NGR	531957, 181811
Local Planning Authority	City of London Corporation
Date built	Late 19th century
Recording note	Recorded in 2011 in advance of demolition to faciltate construction of Crossrail's Farringdon Station eastern ticket hall
Architect	Not known
Builder/Manufacturer	Not known
Original railway company	Partly used by the GWR
Field events	2011, EH Level 2 NLBH record, Scott Wilson Ltd
Bibliography and sources	Crossrail, 2011, *Farringdon Station: Level II Historic Building Record*, C136-SWN-T1-RGN-M123-50002
	London Metropolitan Archives, Smithfields Goods Station, Armour and Company Limited (1916-1959) GLC/AR/BR/22/BA/043620
Site code	XRU10
Archive location	LAARC
Volume reference	p52; CRL Series No.4, p72
Characterisation	Warehouse of seven bays and four storeys. Partly occupied by the GWR during the early 20th century and listed as a printers and bookbinders in 1910. Also used by Armour & Co's meat processing unit in the early to mid 20th century. The building was located above a railway line and a lift was inserted in *c* 1916 to provide access to the platform below.

112: 20-23 Long Lane and 2 Lindsey Street, London EC1

23 Long Lane/2 Lindsey Street (left), 22 Long Lane (middle), 20-21 Long Lane (right) 2009

Monument type	Various, including: CL Commercial, NT Butchers Shop; CL Commercial, NT Temperance Hotel; CL Transport, NT Railway Office
Address	20-23 Long Lane and 2 Lindsey Street, London EC1A 9HL
NGR	531966, 181786
Local Planning Authority	City of London Corporation
Date built	Late 19th century
Recording note	Recorded in 2011 in advance of demolition to facilitate construction of Crossrail's Farringdon Station eastern ticket hall
Architect	Not known
Builder/Manufacturer	Not known
Original railway company	Partly used by the GWR
Field events	2011, EH Level 2 NLBH record, Scott Wilson Ltd
Bibliography and sources	Crossrail, 2011, *Farringdon Station: Level II Historic Building Record*, C136-SWN-T1-RGN-M123-50002
	London Metropolitan Archives, Smithfields Goods Station, Armour and Company Limited (1916-1959) GLC/AR/BR/22/BA/043620
	English Heritage Archives, BL28770/007, Photo of 23 Long Lane (1926)
Site code	XRU10
Archive location	LAARC
Volume reference	p49
Characterisation	In the late 19th century these three buildings were part of the same architectural unit. 23 Long Lane was initially used as a Temperance Hotel. In the early to mid 20th century GWR used 22 Long Lane as a booking and receiving office. By 1926 the meat manufacturers Armour & Co were using 23 Long Lane and 2 Lindsey Street as a wholesale meat shop. In the 1940s they altered 22 Long Lane and 23 Long Lane/2 Lindsey Street. In the 1950s Armour & Co built a bridge that linked 2 Lindsey Street with 8-9 Hayne Street.

115: 101 Moorgate, London EC2

View of 101 Moorgate 2008, facing west

Monument type	CL Commercial, BT Bank (financial); CL Commercial, BT Commercial Office; CL Commercial, BT Shopping Parade
Address	101 Moorgate, London EC2M 6SL
NGR	532720, 181649
Local Planning Authority	City of London Corporation
Date built	1981
Recording note	Recorded in 2008. Demolished during 2011 to facilitate construction of Liverpool Street Station's Moorgate ticket hall
Architect	Maurice Pickering Associates and Trehearnes
Builder/Manufacturer	Trollope and Colls Limited
Field events	None
Bibliography and sources	Crossrail, 2008, *MDC Work Package 3, Archaeological Detailed Desk Based Assessment*, CR-SD-LIV-EN-SR-00001
Site code	None
Archive location	LAARC
Volume reference	p37
Characterisation	Five-storey building with basement. Occupied by AMRO bank and also the firm of Norton Rose, solicitors. Parade of shops at ground-floor level.

117: 11-12 Blomfield Street, London EC2

The Blomfield Street elevation (left 2004), Broad Street Avenue elevation, (right) 2007

Monument type	CL Commercial, BT Commercial Office
Address	11–12 Blomfield Street, London EC2M 7AY
NGR	532993, 181570
Local Planning Authority	City of London Corporation
Date built	1887
Recording note	Recorded in 2010 before demolition to facilitate construction of an emergency shaft for Crossrail
Architect	Not known
Builder/Manufacturer	Not known
Field events	2010, EH Level 2 NLBH record, MOLA
Bibliography and sources	Crossrail, 2011, *11–12 Blomfield Street Standing Building Recording Report*, C257-MLA-X-RGN-CRG03-50001
Site code	XSB10
Archive location	LAARC
Volume reference	p68
Characterisation	Five-storey building used as open plan offices. The Blomfield Street side had a stone facade and a glazed tile entrance with a pediment and a decorative stone urn. The Broad Street facade was plainer and rose to a height of six storeys. Traces of a 19th-century direct acting lift were found below a geometric staircase.

127: Artesian well, Albion Brewery, Whitechapel Road, London E1

Albion Brewery's artesian well 2012

Monument type	CL Water supply and drainage, NT Covered Well
Address	Albion Brewery, 333–335 Whitechapel Road, London E1 1BW
NGR	534878, 181932
Local Planning Authority	Tower Hamlets Council
Date built	Brewery built 1860-68
Recording note	Albion Brewery's building has been retained. The artesian well was backfilled to facilitate Crossrail's construction of Whitechapel Station
Architect	Possibly E N Clifton
Builder/Manufacturer	Building engineer: Robert Spence
Field events	2012, EH Level 2 NLBH record, MOLA
Bibliography and sources	Crossrail, 2012, *Built Heritage Recording Report Level 2 Albion Brewery Well*, C261-MLA-X-RGN-CR140-50099, rev 2
Site code	XSH10
Archive location	LAARC
Volume reference	p58
Characterisation	Albion Brewery entrance block: Grade II listed (list entry no. 1065822). Well located in the basement to the rear of the brewery. Over 200m deep and 2.65m in diameter. Upper section lined with cast iron panels bolted together. Bars and brackets in the upper section could have been for water lifting. The well was designed to extract water from the lower London aquifer.

133: East London Soap Works, Cooks Road, London E15

North-west elevation of the house (left 2009), north-east elevation of the factory (right) 2009

Monument type	CL Industrial, NT Soap Factory
Address	Cooks Road, London E15
NGR	537712, 183289
Local Planning Authority	Newham Council
Date built	Early 20th century
Recording note	Demolished to make way for a Crossrail tunnel portal worksite
Architect	Not known
Builder/Manufacturer	Not known
Field events	2010, EH Level 2 NLBH record, Wessex Archaeology
Bibliography and sources	Crossrail, 2008, *Archaeology Detailed Desk Based Assessment Pudding Mill Lane Portal (including HAM & Wick Sewer Diversion)*, CR-XRL-T1-RGN-CR001-50009;
	Crossrail, 2010, *Pudding Mill Lane Portal Former Works Premises Historic Building Recording*, C262-XRL-T1-RGN-CRG03-50006
Site code	XPM09
Archive location	LAARC
Volume reference	p61
Characterisation	Two buildings were recorded – a factory/workshop with offices and a small house that had been converted to offices. The factory unit had a travelling crane that straddled an internal railway siding. The East London Soap Works 19th-century buildings had been demolished by 1985.

137: The Barge, Victoria Dock Road, Canning Town, London E16

The Barge in 2009, facing north-west

Monument type	CL Commercial, NT Public House
Address	271 Victoria Dock Road, London E16
NGR	540692, 180960
Local Planning Authority	Newham Council
Date built	1862
Recording note	Recorded in 2012 in advance of demolition to facilitate construction of Crossrail's Custom House Station
Architect	Not known
Builder/Manufacturer	Not known
Field events	2013, EH Level 2 NLBH record, MOLA
Bibliography and sources	Crossrail, 2013, C263 *Archaeology Late East Fieldwork Report: Non-Listed Built Heritage The Barge Public House*, C263-MLA-X-RGN-CRG03-50044 Rev 3
Site code	XTI13
Archive location	LAARC
Volume reference	p86
Characterisation	Originally The Freemasons Tavern, renamed in the 1950s. Extension on Freemasons Road added between 1899 and 1919. The second floor was rebuilt in the second half of the 20th century, perhaps after wartime damage.

147: White Hart Depot Power Station, Plumstead, SE18

White Hart Depot main building with cobbled access ramp, facing east 2010

Monument type	CL Industrial, NT Refuse Destructor Station
Address	White Hart Depot, White Hart Road, Plumstead, SE18 1DF
NGR	545399, 178906
Local Planning Authority	Greenwich London Borough Council
Date built	1901-1903
Recording note	Section of approach ramp temporarily removed to facilitate construction of a Crossrail tunnel portal. To be reinstated.
Architect	Designed by Mitchell and Sumner
Builder/Manufacturer	Not known
Field events	2010, EH Level 2 NLBH record, Capita Symonds
Bibliography and sources	Crossrail, 2010, *White Hart Depot, Plumstead Portal Design & Access Statement Listed Building Statement*, C156-CSY-T-RGN-CR148_PT005-00018
Site code	XSJ10
Archive location	LAARC
Volume reference	p43
Characterisation	Grade II Listed Building (entry 1271530). Power station building itself unaffected by Crossrail. However, a section of the external approach ramp has been removed. Granite setts pave the access road and the lower part of the ramp but the upper part of the ramp has been replaced with asphalt. A ramp gradient of 1 in 12.

BIBLIOGRAPHY

Manuscript sources

National Archives

CENSUS RETURNS

1841 Census England and Wales (HO 107)
1851 Census England and Wales (HO 107)
1861 Census England and Wales (RG 9)
1871 Census England and Wales (RG 10)
1881 Census England and Wales (RG 11)
1891 Census England and Wales (RG 12)
1901 Census England and Wales (RG 13)
1911 Census England and Wales (RG 14)
    all accessible online @ www.ancestry.co.uk

WILLS

Prerogative Court of Canterbury wills (1384–1858) (PROB 11)
    accessible online @ www.nationalarchives.gov.uk

London Metropolitan Archives

PARISH REGISTERS AND BURIAL REGISTERS

All Souls Cemetery, Kensall Green, Bishops Transcripts
St George, Bloomsbury (P82/GEO1/016–036)
St James, Clerkenwell (P76/JS1/001–072)
St John, Richmond
St Leonard, Shoreditch (P91/LEN)
    accessible online @ www.ancestry.co.uk

Printed sources

National Probate Calendar 1358-1966 Principal Probate Registry, *Calendar of the Grants of Probate and Letters of Administration made in the Probate Registries of the High Court of Justice in England.* London accessible online @ www.ancestry.co.uk

Secondary works

Baladouni, V, 1990, Charles Lamb: A Man of Letters and a Clerk in the Accountant's Department of the East India Company, The Accounting Historians Journal 17, No.2, 21-36

Ball, M, and Sunderland, D, 2001, *An Economic History of London 1800-1914*, Routledge

Barker, F, and Jackson, P, 1990, *The History of London in Maps*, Guild Publishing, London

Barton, K D, 2008, The Site and Its Surroundings, *Report to the Secretary of State for Communities and Local Government, Development at 43 Farringdon Street, 25 Snow Hill and 29 Smithfield Street*, 3-4

Bills, M, 2008a, Printing & Publishing, in Ross and Clark 2008, 144-45

Bills, M, 2008b, Georgian Art & Artists, in Ross and Clark 2008, 148-49

Bradley, S, & Pevsner, N, 1997, London: City of London Volume 1: The City of London: City of London v. 1 (Pevsner Architectural Guides: Buildings of England) Penguin Books, England

Brandwood, G, Davison, A, and Slaughter, M, 2011, *Licenced To Sell: the history and heritage of the public house*, English Heritage

The Builder, 4 February 1927, 198-203, in Vol CXXXII Jan to June 1927

Cheque and Credit Clearing Company, 2011, Cheques and cheque clearing: An historical perspective, http://www.chequeandcredit.co.uk/files/candc/press/04_cheques_&_cheque_clearing_-_an_historical_perspective_v11_%28may11%29.pdf

City of London, 2014, History of Smithfield Market URL: http://www.cityoflondon.gov.uk/business/wholesale-food-markets/smithfield/Pages/History-of-Smithfield Market.aspx [accessed 15 March 2015]

City of Westminster, nd, *Conservation Area Audit: Soho & Chinatown*

Cox, B, 1994, *English Inn and Tavern Names*, Centre for English Name Studies

Ekwall, E, (ed) 1951, 'Introduction chapter V: the subsidies and the London population, 3, wards and occupations', in Two Early London Subsidy Rolls, pp. 81-87 http://www.british-history.ac.uk/no-series/early-london-subsidy-rolls/pp81-87 [accessed 29 Jan 2015].

Elwall, R, 1983, *Bricks and Beer: English Pub Architecture 1830-1939*, British Architectural Library, London

English Heritage, 1996, *London terrace houses 1660-1860, A guide to alterations and extensions*, Savile Row, London

English Heritage 2006, *Understanding Historic Buildings: A Guide to Good Recording Practice*, EH London

Forsyth, H, 2008a, Printers & Booksellers, in Ross and Clark 2008, 94-95

Forsyth, H, 2008b, The Great Plague, in Ross and Clark 2008, 110-111

Girouard, M, 1984, *Victorian pubs*, Yale University Press

Greeves, I S, 1980, *London Docks 1800-1900: a civil engineering history*, Thomas Telford Ltd

Gorham, M, and Dunnett, H Mc G, 1950, *Inside the Pub*, The Architectural Press, London

Grossmith, G, and Grossmith, W, 1892, *The Diary of a Nobody*, J. W. Arrowsmith Ltd, London

Haigh, G, 2012, *The Office: A Hardworking History*, Miegunyah Press, 2012

Hall, P G, 1962, *The Industries of London*, Hutchinson University Library

Harben, H A, 1918, *A Dictionary of London, Historical notes of streets and buildings in the City of London, including references to other relevant sources*, H Jenkins Ltd, London

Harding, V, & Keene, D J, 1987, All Hallows Honey Lane 11/8, in *Historical Gazetteer of London Before the Great Fire Cheapside*; Parishes of All Hallows Honey Lane, St Martin Pomary, St Mary Le Bow, St Mary Colechurch and St Pancras Soper Lane (London, 1987), pp. 48-78 http://www.british-history. ac.uk/no-series/london-gazetteer-pre-fire/pp48-78 [accessed 26 March 2015]

Harrison, D, 2015 *The Thames Ironworks 1837-1912: A major shipbuilder on the Thames*, Crossrail Archaeology Series 2, Museum of London

Hoffbrand, J, 2008, Sweated Trades & Labour Militancy, in Ross and Clark, 2008, 214-15

Howard, D, 1970, *London Theatres and Music Halls 1850-1950*, The Library Association, London

Jefferies, N with Blackmore, L and Sorapure, D, forthcoming, *Crosse and Blackwell 1830–1920: A British Food Manufacturer in London's West End*, Crossrail Archaeology Series 6

Keily, J, 2008, Trade and Industry in Tudor and Stuart London, in Ross and Clark 2008, 90-91

Latham, M, and Matthews, L, (eds), 1970, *The Diary of Samuel Pepys, Volume II*, 1661, Bell and Sons Ltd, London

Lister, J, 2008, Made in London, in Ross and Clark 2008, 132–33

Marriott, J, 2011, *Beyond the Tower. A History of East London*, Yale UP. London

Maslen, T. J, 1843, *Suggestions for the Improvement of our Towns and Houses*, London

Oliver, B, 1947, *The Renaissance of the English Public House*, Faber and Faber

'One of the Crowd' [James Greenwood] 1883 *Toilers in London*, Diprose & Bateman, London

Peart, S, 1996, *What happened to the cinema near you? Volume 1: Norfolk*, Northacre Publishing

People in Place, 2003, *Families, households and housing in London 1550-1720, Housing and accommodation*, The Institute of Historical Research, URL http://www.history.ac.uk/cmh/pip/pip.html [accessed 10 Feb 2015]

Porter, J F, *c.*1905, *London Pictorially described*, second edition, James B Knapp, Sutton Street, London

Porter, R, 1994, *London. A Social History*, London

Ross, C, 2008a, The Port of Medieval London, in Ross and Clark 2008, 78–9

Ross, C, 2008b, Townhouses & Country homes, in Ross and Clark 2008, 126-127

Ross, C, 2008c, Strangers & Foreigners, in Ross and Clark 2008, 134-135

Ross, C, and Clark, R, (eds.), 2008, *London the Illustrated History,* Museum of London, Penguin Books, London

Saint, A, 2007, 'Shaw, Richard Norman (1831–1912)', Oxford Dictionary of National Biography, Oxford University Press, 2004; online edn, Oct 2007 [http://www.oxforddnb.com/view/article/36050, accessed 25 Feb 2016]

Richard Norman Shaw (1831–1912): doi:10.1093/ref:odnb/36050

Sala, G. A, 1862, *Twice around the Clock*, Richard Marsh, Fleet Street, London

Schofield, J, 2008, A Place of Trade & Industry, in Ross and Clark 2008, 80-1

Sherwell, A., 1901, *Life in West London. A study and a contrast.* 3rd edition, London

Spiller, B, 1972, *Victorian Public Houses*, David and Charles

Summerson, J, 1945, *Georgian London*, Pleiades Books, London

Survey of London, Volumes 33 and 34 St Anne, Soho, ed FHW Shepherd, London, 1966

Thorpe, D, G, H, 2010, A history of British Clearing Banks, British Banking History Society, URL: http://www.banking-history.co.uk/history.html [accessed: 02 April 2014]

Turvey, Ralph, 1993, London Lifts and Hydraulic Power, *Transactions of the Newcomen Society*, 65, 147-164

Werner, A, 2008a, Stocks, Shares & Speculation, in Ross and Clark 2008, 128-129

Werner, A, 2008b, Trade & Industry, in Ross and Clark 2008, 170-171

Werner, A, 2008c, Trains, Trams & The Underground, in Ross and Clark 2008, 212-213

West Ham Borough *c* 1910, *West Ham, the factory centre of the South of England*

Williams, C, (ed) 1933, *Sophie in London 1786: being the diary of Sophie v. la Roche*, translated with an Introduction By C Williams, Jonathan Cape, London

Internet sources

www.arthurlloyd.co.uk/AstoriaTheatreCharingCrossRoad.htm
   (accessed 9 January 2014)

British History Online www.british-history.ac.uk

www.cinematreasures.org/theaters/2499
   (accessed 9 January 2014)

www.heritagepubs.org.uk
   (accessed 18 December 2013)

www.hevac-heritage.org/electronic_books/comfort_AC
   (accessed 14 February 2014)

www.historicengland.org.uk/listing

Locating London's Past www.locatinglondon.org

Old Bailey Online www.oldbaileyonline.org

www.officemuseum.com

Online Historical Population reports www.histpop.org

People in Place, Families, households and housing in London 1550-1720
www.history.ac.uk/cmh/pip/

www.pubshistory.com
(accessed 9 January 2014)

www.screenonline.org.uk/film/cinemas
(accessed 9 January 2014)

www. visionofbritain.org